QUOTES ABOUT CREATIVITY:

Inspirational Thoughts about Creative
Thinking Through the Ages

Other Books by Ellen Palestrant

Nosedive

Johannesburg One Hundred

Remembering Dolores

Have You Ever Had a Hunch? The Importance of Creative Thinking

I Touched a Star in My Dream Last Night

Pretzel on Prozac: The Story of an Immigrant Dog

The World of Glimpse

If You Can Make It, Mr. Harris…So Can I

If You Can Make It, Mr. Harris…So Can I Workbook

Let's Do Hunch

KOPTOE: Transcending Boundaries: The Comrades Marathon

Let's Do Hunch…Creativity Workbook for Individual Participants and Groups.

Conversations About Creativity

QUOTES ABOUT CREATIVITY:

Inspirational Thoughts about Creative
Thinking Through the Ages

Edited & Compiled by Ellen Palestrant

First Edition 2018

10 9 8 7 6 5 4 3 2 1

Library of Congress Control Number: To be assigned
ISBN: 978-0-9998247-4-0   Print
        978-0-9998247-5-7   ebook

epCreative Enterprises
www.EllenPalestrant.com

Cover and Interior Layout: The Printed Page, Phoenix, AZ

Categories: Quotation, Art, Writing, Education, Science, Entertainment, Music, Theater, Filmmaking, Philosophy

Contents

Introduction

I have been collecting quotations for many years from a variety of creative thinkers whom I have come across in my readings. Their thoughts about their lives, their creative processes and philosophies on a wide-range of topics have served as both reinforcements to and advancements of my own thinking on creativity and related topics. I have benefited from and enjoyed my internal conversations with these profound thinkers from the past and the present. I decided therefore, to honor their individual strivings and dedication to what was and is meaningful to them in a book of their quotations about creativity.

I have learned from them and I hope you will too when you reflect on their "Observations & Penguinations". Once again, like in my other books in my Creative Thinking Series, my cast of penguins—who have the malleability of representing human characteristics—have invited themselves into this book.

PART 1.

Observations & Penguinations
FRESHNESS OF VISION:

Childhood
Adulthood
Education
Playfulness
Make-Believe

*Every child is an artist. The problem is
to remain an artist once he grows up.*
—**Pablo Picasso**,
Spanish artist (1881–1973)

My music is best understood by children and animals.
—**Igor Stravinsky**,
Russian composer (1882–1971)

*Man's main task is to give birth to himself,
to become what he potentially is.*
—**Erich Fromm**,
psychoanalyst (1900–1980)

*Looking back, I see that the best thing my parents
did for me was simply not to get in my way. That's
sound advice for a parent trying to encourage an
artistic child. If you can provide him or her with pen,
paper, colors, a table, and a place to work, you've
done it all.*
—**Charles M. Schultz**,
American cartoonist (1922–2000)

*Telling me to take a vacation from film-making is like
telling a child to take a vacation from playing.*
—Stanley Kubrick,
American film director (1928–1999)

*When I look back at my adolescence, I don't remember a
day without sunshine because sunshine was in my soul.*
—Toscanini—Arturo Toscanini,
acclaimed Italian conductor (1867–1957)

*Age is opportunity no less than youth itself,
though in another dress.*
—Henry Wadsworth Longfellow,
American poet (1807–1882)

*Artists can color the sky red because they know it is
blue. Those of us who aren't artists must color things
the way they really are or people might think we're
stupid.*
—Jules Feiffer,
American syndicated cartoonist and author (1929–)

Give me a child and I'll shape him into anything.
—B.F. Skinner,
American behaviorist (1904–1990)

Through spontaneity we are re-formed into ourselves.
It creates an explosion that for the moment frees
us from handed-down frames of reference, memory
choked with old facts and information and undigested
theories and techniques of other people's findings.
—Viola Spolin,
American improvisational educator (1906–1994)

I am one of the few who continue to draw after
childhood is ended, continuing and perfecting
childhood drawing without the traditional
interruptions of academic training.
—Saul Steinberg,
American cartoonist (1908–1973)

When I was four, I could draw as well as Raphael.
It has taken me my whole life to learn to draw like a child.
—Pablo Picasso,
Spanish artist (1881–1973)

Life is not meant to be easy my child;
but take courage: it can be delightful.
—George Bernard Shaw,
Irish writer (1856–1950)

Hardening of the categories causes art disease.
—W. Eugene Smith,
photojournalist (1918–1978)

When I was a child, my mother said to me, "If you
become a soldier, you'll be a general. If you become
a monk, you'll be the pope." I became a painter and
wound up Picasso.
—Pablo Picasso,
Spanish artist (1881–1973)

Creative minds always have been known
to survive any kind of bad training.
—Anna Freud,
Pioneer: child psychoanalysis ((1895–19820)

Do not worry about your difficulties in mathematics;
I can assure you that mine are still greater.
—**Albert Einstein,**
German-born theoretical physicist &
Nobel Laureate (1879–1955)

One can compare art education to the solid
foundation for a house—once it's properly built,
it will hold any shape or form you will place in it.
—**Igor Babailov,**
painter (1965–)

Rhyme is a mnemonic devise, an aid to memory.
—**James Fenton,**
English poet (1949–)

Accommodation to the absurd readmits adults
to the mysterious realm inhabited by children.
—**André Breton,**
French poet & founder of Surrealism (1896–1966)

For the mass in America today, the most powerful medium of education and information has become a surrogate of Linus's blue blanket. A ghastly glass teat.
—**Harlan Ellison,**
American writer (1934–)

If you see in any given situation only what everybody else can see, you can be said to be so much a representative of your culture that you are a victim of it.
—**S.I. Hayakawa,**
Scholar & U.S. senator (1906–19992)

If you get all the facts, your judgment can be right: if you don't get all the facts, it can't be right.
—**Bernard Mannes Baruch,**
American Statesman (1870–1965)

It is a happy talent to know how to play.
—**Ralph Waldo Emerson,**
American poet & essayist (1803–1882)

Even though I appear 93,
I never lost my child-like view of the world.
—Norman Lear,
American television writer & producer (1922–)

The child in me is delighted,
the adult in me is skeptical.
—Saul Bellow,
upon receiving the 1976 Nobel Prize for literature
(1915–2005)

Part 2.

Observations & Penguinations
SUSTAINING FRESHNESS OF VISION

Mystery
Inspiration
Intuition
Imagination
Dreams & Illusions
Ideas
Inventiveness
Aloneness
Collaboration
Process & Abundance

*A writer takes earnest measures to secure
his solitude and then finds endless ways to squander it.*
—De Lilo,
American novelist & playwright (1936–)

Painting is stronger than I am.
It makes me do what it wants.
—Pablo Picasso,
Spanish artist (1881–1973)

*Only when he no longer knows what he is doing
does the painter do good things.*
—Edgar Degas,
French painter and sculptor (1834–1917)

*I don't know in advance what I am going to put on
the canvas any more than I decide beforehand what
colors I am going to use.*
—Pablo Picasso,
Spanish artist (1881–1973)

Every artist dips his brush into his own soul,
and paints his own nature into the picture.
—Henry Ward Bleecher,
American clergyman (1813–1887)

———⌣———

Success is dangerous. One begins to copy oneself,
and to copy oneself is more dangerous than
to copy others. It leads to sterility.
—Pablo Picasso,
Spanish artist (1881–1973)

———⌣———

Say "red"…and there are fifty people listening, it
can be expected that there will be fifty reds in their
minds. And one can be sure that all these reds will be
different.
—Josef Albers,
Artist & educator (1888–1976)

———⌣———

A bird does not sing because it has an answer.
It sings because it has a song.
—Chinese Proverb

———⌣———

Follow the masters!
But why should one follow them?
The only reason they are masters
is that they didn't follow anybody!
—Paul Gauguin,
French artist (1848–1903)

There is a vitality, a life force, a quickening that is
translated through you into action, and because
there is only one of you in all time, this expression
is unique. If you block it, it will never exist through
any other medium and will be lost. The world will
not have it.
—Martha Graham,
American dancer & choreographer (1894–1991)
to Agnes DeMille

The artist never entirely knows.
We guess. We may be wrong,
but we take leap after leap in the dark.
—Agnes de Mille,
American dancer and Choreographer (1905–1993)

Keep the channel open. No artist ever pleased everyone. There is no satisfaction whatever at any time...a blessed unrest that keeps us marching and makes us more alive than others.
—Martha Graham,
American dancer & choreographer (1894–1991) to
Agnes DeMille

The self-denial, the sacrifice that our work demands are all compensated for by that lovely serenity of giving yourself up to dance.
—Edward Villella,
American ballet dancer and choreographer (1936–)

Do not fear yourself, for that is your self.
—Carl Jung,
Swiss psychoanalyst (1875–1961)

*Be what you is, not what you ain't,
'cause if you ain't what you is,
you is what you ain't.*
—Luther D. Price,
philosopher

What oft is thought but n'er well expressed
—Alexander Pope,
English poet (1688–1744)

Everything has been thought of before,
but the problem is to think of it again.
—Goethe,
German writer (1749–1832)

The wise man seeks everything in himself;
the ignorant man tries to get everything
from somebody else.
—Kung Fu,
Chinese martial art

If a man does not keep pace with his companions,
perhaps it is because he hears a different drummer.
Let him step to the music which he hears, however
measured or far away.
—Henry David Thoreau,
American writer & poet (1817–1862)

Sometimes it's better to go a long distance out of the way
in order to come back a short distance correctly.
—Edward Albee,
American playwright (1928–1889)

The job of the artist is always to deepen the mystery.
—Francis Bacon,
painter (1909–1992)

By understanding the unconscious
we free ourselves from its domination.
—Carl Jung,
Swiss psychoanalyst (1875–1961)

Asking an artist to talk about his work
is like asking a plant to discuss horticulture.
—Jean Cocteau,
French writer, artist, filmmaker (1889–1963)

A hunch is creativity trying to tell you something.
—Frank Capra,
film director (1897–1991)

To me, the greatest pleasure of writing is not what it's about, but the inner music that words make.
—**Truman Capote**,
American writer (1924–1984)

The only way that your dream can die is if you kill it yourself. If you do that, you will have condemned yourself along with it.
—**Tom Clancy**,
American novelist (1947–2013)

You're never too old to set another goal or to dream a new dream.
—**C.S. Lewis**,
British novelist & poet (1898–1963)

If I create from the heart, nearly everything works; if from the head, almost nothing.
—**Marc Chagall**,
painter(1889–1985)

Painting must do for the eyes
what poetry does for the ears.
—Antoine Coypel,
painter(1661–1722)

Music is made up of colors and barred rhythms.
—Claude Debussy,
French composer (1862–1918)

The thing that is important is the thing that is not seen.
—De Saint-Exupéry,
French writer, poet, (1900–1944)

An original writer is not one who imitates nobody,
but one whom nobody can imitate.
—François-Rene de Châteaubriand,
French writer (1768–1848)

Any sort of pretension induces mediocrity
in art and life alike.
—Margot Fonteyn,
ballerina with Royal Ballet (1919–1991)

Imitation is not inspiration, and inspiration only can give birth to a work of art. The least of man's original emanations is better than the best of borrowed thought.
—**Albert Pinkham Ryder**,
American painter (1847–1917)

What is thought, is.
What is, is thought.
I travel from spirit to matter.
I return from matter to spirit.
There are no frontiers.
—**Carlos Fuentes**,
"Terra Nostra" Mexican writer (1928–2012)

A sequel is an admission that you have been reduced to imitating yourself.
—**Don Marquis**,
American writer & humorist (1978–1937)

Originality does not consist in saying what no one has ever said before, but in saying exactly what you think yourself.
—**J.F. Stephen**,
British High Court Judge (1829–1894)

Imagination is the eye of the soul.
—Joseph Joubert,
French moralist and essayist (1754–1824)

At every moment where language can't go,
that's your mind.
—Bodhidharma,
Indian Buddhist monk (450–500 AD)

I may not have gone where I intended to go,
but I have ended up where I need to be.
—Douglas Adams,
English writer (1952–2001)

Color which is like music, is is a matter of vibrations,
reaches what is most general and therefore most
undefinable in nature: its inner power.
—Paul Gauguin,
French artist (1848–1903)

In the realm of ideas everything depends on enthusiasm.
—Goethe,
German writer (1749–1832)

*A new idea is a light that illuminates presences which
simply had no form for us before the light fell*
—**Susanne K. Langer,**
American writer & philosopher (1895–1985)

*There are vast realms of consciousness still undreamed
of vast ranges of experience, like the humming of
unseen harps, we know nothing of, within us.*
—**D.H. Lawrence,**
Terra Incognita, English writer & painter (1885–1930)

*Shut off your mind. When the rational mind is shut off,
we have the possibility of intuition.*
—**Viola Spolin,**
American improvisational educator (1906–1994)

Nothing happens unless first a dream.
—**Carl Sandburg,**
Swedish-American poet & writer (1878–1967)

It is only with the heart that one can see rightly;
what is essential is invisible to the eye.
—De Saint-Exupéry
French writer, poet, (1900–1944)

⁓⌣⁓

A rock pile ceases to be a rock pile the moment
a single man contemplates it, bearing within him
the image of a cathedral.
—De Saint-Exupéry,
French writer, poet, (1900–1944)

⁓⌣⁓

Art is the opposite of nature.
A work of art can come only from the interior of man.
—Edvard Munch,
Norwegian artist (1863–1944)

⁓⌣⁓

I trust in inspiration, which sometimes comes
and sometimes doesn't.
But I don't sit back waiting for it.
I work every day.
—Alberto Moravia,
Italian novelist (1907–1990)

⁓⌣⁓

The passion of the artist is humble.
He is essentially a channel.
—**Piet Mondrian**,
Dutch artist (1872–1944)

The difference between painting and other forms of
creativity like writing or filmmaking is that painting
is a preverbal experience…an experience without the
aid of knowing what the experience is without words
already formed to describe it.
—**Piet Mondrian**,
Dutch artist (1872–1944)

There are flowers everywhere,
for those who bother to look.
—**Henri Matisse**,
French artist (1869–1954)

Art enables us to find ourselves and
lose ourselves at the same time.
—**Thomas Merton**,
American writer & theologian (1915–1968)

*My own experience of inspiration...a dim cloud of an idea
which I feel must be condensed into a shower of words.*
—Stephen Spender,
English poet & novelist (1909–1995)

*Noise...is not only an interruption
but also a disruption of thought.*
—Arthur Schopenhauer,
German philosopher (1788–1860)

Somewhere something incredible is waiting to be known.
—Carl Sagan,
American writer, & astronomer (1934–1996)

*Imagination will often carry us to worlds that
never were, but without it we go nowhere.*
—Carl Sagan,
American writer, & astronomer (1934–1996)

*Music (is) a form of communion with
our fellow man and with the Supreme Being.*
—Igor Stravinsky,
Russian composer (1882–1971)

*Writing is perhaps the greatest of human inventions,
binding together people, citizens of distant epochs,
who never knew one another. Books break the
shackles of time, proof that humans can work magic.*
—**Carl Sagan**,
American writer, & astronomer (1934–1996)

Vision is the art of seeing the invisible.
—**Jonathan Swift**,
Anglo-Irish satirist (1667–1745)

Seeing is the art of seeing what is invisible to others.
—**Jonathan Swift**,
Anglo-Irish satirist (1667–1745)

*We work in our darkness a great deal with little
knowledge of what we are doing.*
—**John Steinbeck**,
American writer & Nobel Laureate (1902–1968)

The good writer always aims at the impossible.
—**John Steinbeck**,
American writer & Nobel Laureate (1902–1968)

Any plan is bad which is not susceptible to change.
—Bartolommeo De San Concordio,
Florentine painter & writer (1260–1347)

*When you use a fish you don't think of its scales,
do you? You think of its speed, its floating, flashing
body seen through the water. Well I've tried to
express just that…the flash of its spirit.*
—Constantine Brancusi,
French painter & sculptor (1976–1957)

*There is only one valuable thing in art:
the thing you cannot explain.*
—Georges Braque,
French painter & sculptor (1882–1963)

*Anything that has real and lasting value
is always a gift from within.*
—Franz Kafka,
Bohemian writer (1883–1924)

Art is a delayed echo
—**George Santayana**,
Spanish writer & philosopher (1863–1952)

Freedom from the desire for an answer
is essential to the understanding of a problem.
—**Jiddu Krishnamurti**,
Indian theosophist (1895–1986)

I very much loved...the feeling of bringing...
totally unrelated...areas of my life together
as one can in fiction.
—**John Cheever**,
American writer (1912–1982)

If a poet has pursued a moral objective,
he has diminished his poetic force.
—**Charles-Pierre Baudelaire**,
French poet, translator (1821–1867)

Many characters have come to me...in a dream,
and then I'll elaborate from there.
I always write down all my dreams.
—**William Burroughs**,
American author (1914–1997)

You never have to change anything
you get up in the middle of the night to write.
—Saul Bellow,
writer & Nobel Laureate (1915–2005)

They who dream by day are cognizant of many things
which escape those who dream only by night.
—Edgar Allan Poe,
American writer & poet (1809–1849)

Why do colors, put one next to the other, sing?
Can one really explain this? No.
—Pablo Picasso,
Spanish artist (1881–1973)

An imaginative novelist's greatest virtue is his
ability to forget the world in a way a child does, to be
irresponsible and delight in it, to play around with
the rules of the known world—but at the same time
to see past his freewheeling flights of fancy to the
deep responsibility of later allowing readers to lose
themselves in the story.
—Orhan Pamuk,
Turkish writer and Nobel Laureate (1952–)

*There are painters who transform the sun to a yellow
spot, but there are others who with the help of their
intelligence, transform a yellow spot into sun.*
—**Pablo Picasso**,
Spanish artist (1881–1973)

Every hour of the light and dark is a miracle.
—**Walt Whitman**
Leaves of Grass, American poet & essayist (1819–1892)

Always be on the lookout for the presence of wonder.
—**E.B. White**,
American writer (1899–1985)

In search of my mother's garden, I found my own.
—**Alice Walker**,
American writer (1944–)

*The music in my heart I bore
Long after it was heard no more.*
—**William Wordsworth**,
English poet (1770–1850)

*Reality only exists when it is
illuminated by a ray of poetry.*
—Georges Braque,
French painter & sculptor (1882–1963)

This world is but a canvas to our imagination.
—Henry David Thoreau,
American writer & poet (1817–1862)

*Imagination is more important than knowledge. For
knowledge is limited, whereas imagination embraces
the entire world, stimulating progress, giving birth
to evolution.*
—Albert Einstein,
theoretical physicist, philosopher & Nobel Laureate
(1879–1955)

*If at first the idea is not absurd,
then there is no hope for it.*
—Albert Einstein,
theoretical physicist, philosopher & Nobel Laureate (1879–1955)

Fantasy is hardly an escape from reality.
It is a way of understanding it.
—**Lloyd Alexander**,
American writer (1924–2007)

Imagination, imagination, imagination!
It converts to actual. It sustains, it alters, it redeems!"
—**Saul Bellow**,
writer, Nobel Laureate (1915–2005)

Ideas excite me, and as soon as I get excited, the
adrenaline gets going and the next thing I know I'm
borrowing energy from the ideas themselves.
—**Ray Bradbury**,
American writer (1920–2012)

Inspiration comes to me unexpectedly,
never by virtue of deliberate stimulation,
never by sitting in a chair:
it always happens in front of my easel.
—**William Baziotes**,
American painter (1912–1963)

A book is like a garden carried in the pocket.
—**Chinese Proverb**

A bird does not sing because it has an answer.
It sings because it has a song.
—**Chinese Proverb**

To stop the flow of music would be like
stopping time itself, incredible and inconceivable.
—**Aaron Copland,**
American composer (1900–1990)

Color is the keyboard, the eyes are the hammers, the
soul is the piano with many strings. The artist is the
hand that plays…to cause vibrations in the soul.
—**Wassily Kandinsky,**
Russian abstract artist *(1866–1944)*

Always be a poet, even in prose.
—**Charles-Pierre Baudelaire,**
French poet, translator (1821–1867)

A sagious student does not depend on his teacher's words
but uses his experience to find the truth.
—**Bodhidharma**,
Indian Buddhist monk (450–500 AD)

When your own tooth aches, you know how to
sympathize with one who has a toothache.
—**Chinese proverb**

Imagination is the only weapon
in the war against reality.
—**Lewis Carroll**,
English writer (1832–1898)

The sea, once it has cast its spell,
holds one in the net of wonder forever.
—**Jacques Yves Cousteau**,
filmmaker & explorer (1910–1997)

*All in all the creative act is not formed by the
artist alone; the spectator brings the work in
contact with the external world by deciphering and
interpreting its inner qualifications and thus adds
his contribution to the creative act.*
—**Marcel Duchamp**,
French painter & writer (1887–1968)

*Paintings must be looked at and looked at and looked at…
No writing, no singing, no dancing will explain them.*
—**Charles Demuth**,
American painter *(1883–1935)*

*To be understood a writer has to explain
almost everything. In a painting, a mysterious bridge
seems to exist between the painted subjects
and the spectator's spirit.*
—**Eugène Delacroi**x,
French painter (1796–1863)

The first merit of a picture is to be a feast for the eyes.
—**Eugène Delacroix**,
French painter (1796–1863)

The most beautiful experience we can have is the mysterious—the fundamental emotion which stands at the cradle of true art and true science.
—**Albert Einstein,**
German-born theoretical physicist & Nobel Laureate
(1879–1955)

There are things that I have seen
Although I have not been
To where they are…
—**R.H.W. Dillard,**
American poet & writer (1937–)

I used to go for weeks in a state of confusion.
—**Albert Einstein,**
German-born theoretical physicist & Nobel Laureate
(1879–1955)

The intellect has little to do on the road to discovery. There comes a leap in consciousness, call it intuition or what you will, and the solution comes to you and you don't know how or why.
—**Albert Einstein,**
German-born theoretical physicist & Nobel Laureate
(1879–1955)

*The value of a man should be seen in
what he gives and not in what he is able to receive.*
—**Albert Einstein**,
German-born theoretical physicist & Nobel Laureate
(1879–1955)

Each should follow where the pulse of his own heart leads.
—**Paul Klee**,
Swiss-born painter (1879–1940)

*One day I must be able to improvise freely
on the keyboard of colours:
the row of watercolours in my paintbox.*
—**Paul Klee**,
Swiss-born painter (1879–1940)

*After silence, that which comes nearest
to expressing the inexpressible is music.*
—**Aldous Huxley**,
English writer & philosopher (1894–1963)

The best kind of conversation
is that which may be called thinking aloud.
—William Hazlett,
English writer & painter (1178–1830)

∼⌢∽

No amount of skillful invention
can replace the essential element of imagination.
—Edward Hopper,
American painter (1882–1967)

∼⌢∽

I'm at the service of the material that enters me.
It takes me where it wants to go.
—Russell Hoban,
American writer (1925–2011)

∼⌢∽

More of me comes out when I improvise.
—Edward Hopper,
American artist (1882–1967)

∼⌢∽

I begin with an idea and then it becomes something else.
—Pablo Picasso,
Spanish artist (1881–1973)

∼⌢∽

You have to have an idea of what you are going to do,
but it should be a vague idea.
—**Pablo Picasso**,
Spanish artist (1881–1973)

⁓⌒⁓

The world of reality has its limits;
the world of imagination is boundless.
—**Jean-Jacques Rousseau**,
Francophone philosopher (1712–1778)

⁓⌒⁓

There are so many possibilities,
it's downright incredible.
—**Gerhard Richter**,
German artist (1932–)

⁓⌒⁓

The happiness that is genuinely satisfying is
accompanied by the fullest exercise of our faculties,
and the fullest realization of the world in which we live.
—**Bertrand Russell**,
British philosopher (1872–1970)

⁓⌒⁓

*I put my trust in the materials that confront me,
because they put me in touch with the unknown.*
—**Robert Rauschenberg,**
American painter (1925–2008)

*A young artist must forget painting when he paints.
That's the only way he'll do original work.*
—**Pablo Picasso,**
Spanish artist (1881–1973)

*To blossom forth, a work of art must ignore
or rather forget all the rules.*
—**Pablo Picasso,**
Spanish artist (1881–1973)

*If you hear a voice within you say 'you cannot paint,'
then by all means paint and that voice will be silenced.*
—**Vincent van Gogh,**
Dutch Post-Impressionist painter (1853–1890)

I dream my painting and then I paint my dream.
—**Vincent van Gogh,**
Dutch Post-Impressionist painter (1853–1890)

Everyone wants to understand art.
Why not try to understand a bird?
—**Pablo Picasso,**
Spanish artist (1881–1973)

Ideas are like rabbits. You get a couple and
learn how to handle them,
and pretty soon you have a dozen.
—**John Steinbeck,**
American writer (1902–1968)

Writers don't have lifestyles.
They sit in little rooms and write.
—**Norman Mailer,**
American novelist writer (1923–2007)

Begin, be bold, and venture to be wise.
—**Horace,**
Roman, Latin-speaking poet (8, 65 BC–27, 8 BC)

Mistakes are the portals for discovery.
—**James Joyce,**
Irish writer (1882–1941)

Light shone, and order from disorder sprung.
—**John Milton,**
English poet (1608–1674)

When I am, as it were, completely myself, entirely alone… my ideas flow best and most abundantly.
—**Wolfgang Amadeus Mozart,**
Austrian composer (1756–1791)

All things are in motion and nothing is at rest… you cannot go into the same river twice.
—**Heraclitus,**
Greek philosopher (500 BCE)

Painting is poetry that is seen rather than felt, and poetry is painting that is felt rather than seen.
—**Leonardo Da Vinci,**
Renaissance, inventor & artist (1452–1519)

Nothing will change the fact that I cannot produce the least thing without absolute solitude.
—**Goethe,**
German writer (1749–1832)

The best way to have a good idea is to have lots of ideas.
—Linus Pauling,
American biochemist (1901–1994)

Technique alone is never enough.
You have to have passion.
Technique alone is just an embroidered potholder.
—Raymond Chandler,
American novelist (1888–1959)

The need to write comes from the need to make sense
of one's life and discover one's usefulness.
—John Cheever,
American writer (1912–1982)

No one can arrive from being talented alone,
work transforms talent into genius.
—Anna Pavlova,
Russian prima ballerina (1881–1931)

Treat a work of art like a prince. Let it speak first.
—**Arthur Schopenhauer**,
German philosopher (1788–1860)

Loneliness is your companion for life.
If you don't want to be lonely, you get into TV.
—**William Styron**,
American novelist (1925–2006)

The writer works in a lonely way.
—**Irwin Shaw**,
American writer (1913–1984)

Truly creative people usually are loners working in their
own way at their own pace on their own subjects.
—**Robert C. Schank**,
American A.I. theorist (1946–)

Not I, not anyone else can travel the road for you,
You must travel it for yourself.
—**Walt Whitman**,
Song of Myself, American poet & essayist (1819–1892)

Solitude is blankness that makes accidents happen.
—Robert Penn Warren,
American poet and novelist (1905–1989)

It is a mistake to think that the practice of my art has become easy to me. I assure you, dear friend, no one has given so much care to the study of composition as I. There is scarcely a famous master in music whose works I have not frequently and diligently studied.
—Wofgang Amadeus Mozart,
Austrian composer (1756–1791)

I think there are certain forms of creativity that demand the work of one single person, whether it is a person sitting at a drawing board, a person sitting at a piano, or a person sitting behind an easel painting. And I think comic strips are drawn by one dedicated person sitting all by himself in a room at a drawing board.
—Charles M. Schultz,
American cartoonist (1922–2000)

Spontaneity is the moment of personal freedom when we are faced with reality and see it, explore it and act accordingly.
—Viola Spolin,
American improvisational educator (1906–1994)

Sometimes it is more important to discover
what one cannot do than what one can do
—**Lin Yutang,**
Chinese writer, translator, linguist and inventor (1895–1976)

Everything seems an echo of something else.
—**Robert Penn Warren,**
American writer (1905–1989)

A picture is finished when all trace of the means
used to bring about the end has disappeared.
—**James Abott McNeill Whistler**
American artist (1834–1903)

What can any of us do with his talent but try to
develop his vision, so that through frequent failures
we may learn better what we have missed in the past.
—**William Carlos Williams,**
American poet (1833–1963)

The minute I sat in front of a canvas, I was happy.
Because it was a world, and I could do as I liked in it.
—**Alice Neel**,
American artist (1900–1984)

⌒⌒

Talent is a mastery of quantity:
talent doesn't write one page, it writes three hundred.
—**Jules Renard**,
French writer (1864–1910)

⌒⌒

The difference between the right word
and the almost right word is the difference
between lightning and a lightning bug.
—**Mark Twain**,
writer & humorist (1835–1910)

⌒⌒

It is not enough to be busy…
The question is what are we busy about?
—**Henry David Thoreau**,
American writer & poet (1817–1862)

⌒⌒

*Nothing is a waste of time
if you use the experience wisely.*
—**Auguste Rodin**,
French sculptor (1840–1917)

⁓⁓⁓

*If I have ever made any valuable discoveries, it has been
owing more to patient attention than to any other talent.*
—**Isaac Newton**,
English mathematician & physicist (1642–1727)

⁓⁓⁓

*I always have at the very start a curiously clear
preview of the entire novel before me or above me.*
—**Vladimir Nabokov**,
Russian-American novelist (1899–1977)

⁓⁓⁓

*The idea came to me without anything in my former
thoughts seeming to pave the way for it....*
—**Henri Poincare**,
The Foundations of Science,
French mathematician & physicist (1854–1912)

⁓⁓⁓

*I don't know about method.
The* what *is so much more important than how.*
—**Ezra Pound**,
Expatriate American poet (1885–1972)

*Happy accidents are real gifts, and they can
open the door to a future that didn't even exist.*
—David Lynch,
American artist and film director, (1946–)

*Telling me to take a vacation from film-making
is like telling a child to take a vacation from playing.*
—Stanley Kubrick,
American film director (1928–1999)

*The artist who aims at perfection
in everything achieves it in nothing.*
—Eugène Delacroix,
French painter (1796–1863)

*On many occasions,
where you are going is exactly where you are.*
—Norton Juster,
writer "The Phantom Tollbooth" (1929–)

If you are possessed by an idea,
you find it expressed everywhere, you even smell it.
—**Thomas Mann**,
German writer & Nobel Prize Laureate (1875–1955)

⁓⸱⁓

Finally I am coming to the conclusion
that my highest ambition is to be what I already am.
—**Thomas Merton**,
American writer & theologian (1915–1968)

⁓⸱⁓

As long as I can conceive something better than
myself I cannot be easy unless I am striving to bring
it into existence or clearing the way for it. That is the
law of my life.
—**George Bernard Shaw**,
Irish writer (1856–1950)

⁓⸱⁓

There is no right or wrong way to solve a problem;
there is only one way—the seeking—in which one
learns by going through the process itself.
—**Viola Spolin**,
American improvisational educator (1906–1994)

⁓⸱⁓

I always know the ending; that's where I start.
—Toni Morrison,
American writer (1931–)

───~·~───

Dare we do bad works often they are the best in such a sense bad is only external but inwardly the artist feels new depths and he is already there where the others are not or may not be for a generation.
—David Smith,
Sculptor & painter(1906–1965)

───~·~───

I like to compare my method with that of painters centuries ago, proceeding from layer to layer.
—Alberto Moravia,
Italian novelist (1907–1990)

───~·~───

Usually I begin a poem with an image or phrase; if you follow trustfully, it's surprising how far an image can lead.
—James Merrill,
American poet (1926–1995)

───~·~───

*The colors live a remarkable life of their own
after they have been applied to the canvas.*
—Edvard Munch,
Norwegian artist (1863–1944)

*I found I could say things with color and shapes
that I couldn't say in any other way—
things that I had no words for.*
—Georgia O' Keefe,
American artist (1888–1976)

*Color is one of the great things in the world
that makes it worth living for me…
(I) paint color for the world—life as I see it.*
—Georgia O' Keefe,
American artist (1888–1976)

*To me it was not a matter of how I became a cartoonist
but a matter of when. I am quite sure if I had not
sold* **Peanuts** *at the time I did, then I would have
sold something eventually. Even if I had not, I would
continue to draw because I had to.*
—Charles M. Schultz,
American cartoonist (1922–2000)

I have found drawing with pen and ink to be very challenging as well as gratifying. I feel that it is possible to achieve something near to what fine artists call 'paint quality' when working with pen.
—**Charles M. Schultz,**
American cartoonist (1922–2000)

To create something out of nothing is a wonderful experience.
—**Charles M. Schultz,**
American cartoonist (1922–2000)

Anyone involved in anything creative has to be putting a lot of himself into it. I would say all the characters are me in one form or another.
—**Charles M. Schultz,**
American cartoonist (1922–2000)

The guitar is a small orchestra. Every string is a different color.
—**Andrea Segovia,**
Spanish Classical Guitarist (1893–1987)

Writing is like a contact sport, like football,
you can get hurt, but you enjoy it.
—Irwin Shaw,
American writer (1913–1984)

Color is like music. The palette is an instrument
that can be orchestrated to build form.
—John Sloan,
American artist (1871–1951)

Don't judge each day by the harvest you reap,
But by the seeds you plant.
—Robert Louis Stevenson,
poet & novelist (1850–1894)

Cultural confinement takes place when a curator
imposes his own limits on an art exhibition, rather
than asking an artist to set his limits.
—Robert Smithson,
American artist, photographer, sculptor (1938–1973)

*Specialist: a man who knows
more and more about less and less.*
—**Dr. William J. Mayo**,
one of the founders of the Mayo Clinic (1861–1939)

*In a conflict between the heart and the brain,
follow your heart.*
—**Swami Vivekananda**,
Indian Hindu monk (1863–1902)

*You don't start with an aesthetic manifesto,
you just do what works.*
—**E.L. Doctorow (Edgar Lawrence)**
American novelist, editor, and professor (1931–2015)

*Freedom from the desire for an answer
is essential to the understanding of a problem.*
—**Jiddu Krishnamurti**,
Indian theosophist (1895–1986)

We shall not cease from exploration
And the end of all our exploring
Will be where we started
And know the place for the first time.
—**T.S. Eliot**,
British poet & playwright (1888–1965)

~———~

Prose is words in their best order;
poetry is the best words in the best order
—**Samuel Taylor Coleridge**
English poet (1772–1834)

~———~

Always be a poet, even in prose.
—**Charles-Pierre Baudelaire**,
French poet, translator (1821–1867)

~———~

Words are made for a certain exactness of thought,
as tears for a certain degree of pain.
—**Renee Daumal**,
French writer & poet (1908–1944)

~———~

It seems that perfection is attained not when there is nothing more to add, but when there is nothing more to take away.
—De Saint-Exupéry,
French writer, poet, aristocrat

Ideas came into my mind quite unrelated to graphic art, notions which so fascinated me that I longed to communicate them to other people. This could not be achieved through words…but mental images of a kind that can only be made comprehensible to others by presenting them as visual images.
—M.C. Escher,
Dutch graphic artist (1898–1972)

Many of life's failures are people who did not realize how close they were to success when they gave up.
—Thomas A. Edison,
inventor (1847–1931)

The value of an idea lies in the using of it.
—Thomas A. Edison,
inventor (1847–1931)

I find out what the world needs.
Then I go ahead and try to invent it.
—Thomas A. Edison,
inventor (1847–1931)

~

There are infinite modes of expression in the world of art, and to insist that only by one road can the artist attain his ends is to limit him.
—Jacob Epstein,
sculptor (1880–1959)

~

Age is opportunity no less than youth itself,
though in another dress.
—Henry Wadsworth Longfellow,
American poet (1807–1882)

~

The best thing one can do
when it's raining is to let it rain.
—Henry Wadsworth Longfellow,
American poet (1807–1882)

~

If at first you don't succeed, try, try again.
Then quit. No use being a damn fool about it.
—W.C. Fields,
American comedian & writer (1880–1946)

The years of my life that went into the book were not
years of thinking but of feeling, wordless brooding.
—William Golding,
British writer & Nobel Laureate (1911–1993)

Art is work
—Milton Glazer,
American artist (1929–)

It is hard to convince people when you're just staring
out of the window that you are doing your hardest
work of the day. In fact, many times when I'm sitting
here thinking and therefore really working, I hear
the door open and I quickly grab the pen and a piece
of paper and start drawing something and so people
won't think I'm just goofing off and anxious to have
a little chat.
—Charles M. Schultz,
American cartoonist (1922–2000)

Life is a lot like jazz…it's best when you improvise.
   —**George Gershwin**,
   American composer (1898–1937)

In some metaphysical way art can reach people and join them in a community of common understanding and purpose.
   —**Milton Glazer**,
   American artist (1929–)

Being alone is one of the most difficult things to learn… you can't succeed if you can't spend time by yourself.
   —**Tom Robbins**,
   American novelist (1932–)

To walk inside yourself and meet no one for hours— that is what you must be able to attain.
   —**Rainer Maria Rilke**,
   Austrian poet (1875–1926)

One must let the play happen to one...
to sense rather than to know,
to gather rather than immediately understand.
—Edward Albee,
American playwright (1928–1889)

I have found that every experience
is a form of exploration.
—Ansel Adams,
American photographer (1902–1984)

The tough thing about success
is that you've got to keep on being a success.
—Irving Berlin,
Russian-born American composer (1888–1989)

Do not try to shortchange the Muse.
It cannot be done. You can't fake quality
any more than you can fake a good meal.
—William Burroughs,
American author (1914–1997)

*It is by sitting down to write every
morning that one becomes a writer.
Those who do not do this remain amateurs.*
—**Gerald Brenan,**
British writer (1894–1987)

Art is the marriage of the conscious and the unconscious.
—**Jean Cocteau,**
French writer, artist, filmmaker (1889–1963)

*My advice to young filmmakers is this:
don't follow trends, start them!*
—**Frank Capra,**
film director (1897–1991)

*Writing has laws of perspective,
of light and shade just as a painting or music*
—**Truman Capote,**
American writer (1924–1984)

To be great is to be misunderstood.
—**Ralph Waldo Emerson,**
American essayist & poet (1803–1882)

*In every work of genius
we recognize our own rejected thoughts.*
—**Ralph Waldo Emerson,**
American poet & essayist (1803–1882)

*Great discoveries and achievements invariably
involve the cooperation of many minds.*
—**Alexander G. Bell,**
Scottish-born American inventor (1847–1922)

*Ideas enlarge the mind and never allow
it to go back to its original dimension.*
—**Chinese Proverb**

*For me, the most important thing is the element
of chance that is built into a live performance.*
—**Aaron Copland,**
American composer (1900–1990)

*You leave the here and now and instead cross over to a
yonder that can be total affirmation, Abstraction.*
—**Paul Klee,**
Swiss-born painter (1879–1940)

⁓⌒

Color possesses me....Color and I are one. I am a painter.
—Paul Klee,
Swiss-born painter (1879–1940)

⁓⌒

The one absolute requirement for me to write...
is to be awake.
—Isaac Asimov,
Science writer & biochemist (1920–1992)

⁓⌒

If my doctor told me I had only six minutes to live,
I wouldn't brood. I'd type a little faster.
—Isaac Asimov,
Science writer & biochemist (1920–1992)

⁓⌒

Far away there in the sunshine are my highest
aspirations. I may not reach them, but I can look
up and see their beauty, believe in them, and try to
follow where they lead.
—Louisa May Alcott,
American novelist & poet (1832–1888)

⁓⌒

Nature is imbued with a rhythm that in its multiplicity cannot be constrained. Art should imitate it in this, in order to purify itself to the height of sublimity, to raise itself to visions of multiple harmony, a harmony of colors separating and coming together again in the same action, This synchronic action is the actual and only subject of painting.
—**Paul Klee**,
Swiss-born painter (1879–1940)

To photograph truthfully and effectively is to see beneath the surfaces.
—**Ansel Adams**,
American photographer (1902–1984)

If you're not failing every now and again, it's a sign you're not doing anything innovative.
—**Woody Allen**,
American writer & filmmaker (1935–)

Creativity is allowing yourself to make mistakes. Art is knowing which ones to keep.
—**Scott Adams**,
American cartoonist and author (1957–)

*If you get all the facts, your judgment can be right:
if you don't get all the facts, it can't be right.*
—Bernard Mannes Baruch,
American Statesman (1870–1965)

*It is hard to compose but what is fabulously hard is to
leave the superfluous notes under the table.*
—Johannes Brahms
German composer (1833–1897)

*Once a novel gets going and I know it is viable, I
don't then worry about plot or themes. These things
will come in almost automatically because the
characters are now pulling the story.*
—Chinua Achebe
Nigerian novelist & poet (1930–2013)

*In my writing I am acting as a map maker,
an explorer of psychic areas,
a cosmonaut of inner space.*
William Burroughs,
American author (1914–1997)

Is there a person who has not made one error
and half a mistake?
—Chinese proverbial wisdom

Not enjoyment, and not sorrow,
Is our destined end or way;
But to act, that each tomorrow
Finds us further than today.
—Henry Wadsworth Longfellow,
American poet (1807–1882)

A journey of a thousand miles
must begin with a single step.
—Chinese Proverb

Each time dawn appears,
the mystery is there in it's entirety.
—Renee Daumal,
French writer & poet (1908–1944)

Everything in the universe goes by indirection.
There are no straight lines.
—Ralph Waldo Emerson,
American poet & essayist (1803–1882)

Do not go where the path may lead,
go instead where there is no path and leave a trail.
—**Ralph Waldo Emerson**,
American poet & essayist (1803–1882)

Great works are performed
not by strength but by perseverance.
—**Samuel Johnson**,
writer & lexicographer (1709–1784)

Take something.
Do something to it,
Do something else on it.
—**Jasper Johns**,
American artist (1930–)

Perhaps you will discover that you are called to be
an artist. Then take the destiny upon yourself, and
bear it, its burden and its greatness, without ever
asking what reward might come from outside. For
the creator must be a world for himself and must find
everything in himself and in Nature.
—**Rainer Maria Rilke**,
Austrian poet (1875–1926)

It's also always hopeless to talk about painting—
one never does anything but talk around it.
—Francis Bacon,
painter (1909–1992)

Do not finish your work too much.
—Paul Gauguin,
French artist (1848–1903)

It's never a problem figuring out what to do next.
What you discover in one painting
compels you to do the next.
—George D. Green,
American artist (1943–)

There is no 'must' in art,
Because art is free.
—Wassily Kandinsky,
Russian abstract artist (1866–1944)

The artist must train not only his eye but also his soul."
—Wassily Kandinsky,
Russian abstract artist (1866–1944)

The true work of art is born from the "artist":
a mysterious, enigmatic, and mystical creation…
it acquires an autonomous life.
                    —Wassily Kandinsky,
              Russian abstract artist (1866–1944)

I began to do sculpture because that was precisely the
realm in which I understood least. I couldn't endure
having it elude me completely.
                    —Alberto Giacometti,
              Swiss sculptor (1901–1966)

But the truth is, it's not the idea,
it's never the idea, it's always what you do with it.
                    —Neil Gaiman,
              English writer (1960-)

To rest upon a formula is a slumber
that prolonged, means death.
                    —Oliver Wendell Holmes Jr.,
              U.S. Supreme Court Justice (1841–1935)

Man's mind, once stretched by a new idea, never regains its original dimensions.
—Oliver Wendell Holmes Jr.,
U.S. Supreme Court Justice (1841–1935)

I have no fear of making changes, destroying the image, etc., because the painting has a life of its own.
—Jackson Pollock,
American painter (1912–1956)

I am only a public entertainer who has understood his time.
—Pablo Picasso,
Spanish artist (1881–1973)

I know very dimly when I start what's going to happen. I just have a very general idea and then the thing develops as I write.
—Aldous Huxley,
English writer & philosopher (1894–1963

*I like to listen. I have learned a great deal
from listening carefully. Most people never listen.*
—**Ernest Hemingway**,
American writer (1899–1961)

*The only way to get rid of my fears
is to make films about them.*
—**Alfred Hitchcock**,
English film director (1899–1980)

*Forms develop and grow by themselves....
Sometimes I start with a theme,
but always it gets out of hand.*
—**Hundertwasser**,
Austrian-New Zealand artist (1928–2000)

*You are a lone master;
paint and canvas and you in a room.*
—**Hundertwasser**,
Austrian-New Zealand artist (1928–2000)

The real artist's work is a surprise to himself.
—**Robert Henri**,
American painter (1865–1929)

Art is a habit-forming drug.
—**Marcel Duchamp**,
French painter & writer(1887–1968)

*There are pictures that manifest education
and there are pictures that manifest love.*
—**Robert Henri**,
American painter (1865–1929)

PART 3

Observations & Penguinations
DEFENDING FRESHNESS OF VISION:

Negativity
Judgment
Evaluation
Criticism
Dogmatism
The Thought Patrols

If the only tool you *have is a hammer,*
you treat everything like a nail.
—**Abraham Maslow**,
American psychologist (1908–1970)

Violence is the last refuge of the incompetent.
—**Isaac Asimov**,
Science writer & biochemist (1920–1992)

Liberated from an ideology I looked around at
the world I was in and found myself besieged by
ideologies. Rival ideas...laying claim to the world,
including to myself.
—**Lionel Abrahams**,
South African writer & publisher (1928–2004)

Most of the advice we receive from others...
is evidence of their affection for themselves.
—**Josh Billings**,
American writer (1818–1885)

Get all negative people out of your life.
They're their own funeral.
—Ray Bradbury,
American writer (1920–2012)

⌒⌒⌒

Dogmas always die of dogmatism.
—Annis Nin,
Paris-born American writer (1903–1977)

⌒⌒⌒

You can kill a man but you can't kill an idea.
—Medgar Evers,
Civil rights activist (1925–assassinated in1963)

⌒⌒⌒

There are good people and bad people in every
community. No human race is superior; no religious
faith is inferior. We all come from somewhere and we
all wonder where we are going.
—Elie Wiesel,
Holocaust survivor & Nobel laureate (1928–2016)

⌒⌒⌒

*Human beings are perhaps never more frightening
than when they are convinced beyond doubt
that they are right.*
—Laurens van der Post,
South African novelist & travel writer (1906–1996)

Where all think alike, no one thinks very much.
—Walter Lippmann,
American reporter & political commentator (1889–1974)

His **(Lord Byron***) versification is so destitute
of sustained harmony, many of his thoughts are
so strained, his sentiments so unamiable, his
misanthropy so gloomy, his libertinism so shameless,
his merriment such a grinning of a ghastly smile,
that I always believed his verses would soon rank
with forgotten things.*
—John Quincy Adams,
American statesman (1767–1848)

Mockery is a rust that corrodes all it touches.
—Milan Kundera,
Czech-French writer (1929–)

When a man is unable to understand a thing,
he ridicules it.
—Leo Tolstoy,
Russian writer (1828–1910)

Nobody can make you feel inferior without your consent.
—Eleanor Roosevelt,
American First Lady & diplomat (1884–1862)

We cannot name one considerable poem of his
(**Samuel Taylor Coleridge**) *that is likely to remain*
upon the thresh-floor of fame.
—London Weekly Review–1828

If the critics say your work stinks it's because they
want it to stink and they can make it stink by scaring
you into conformity with their comfortable standards.
—Jack Kerouac,
French-Canadian writer (1922–1969)

John Osborne's Look Back in Anger...
aims at being a despairing cry but achieves
only the stature of a self-pitying snivel.
—Evening Standard

⌒‿⌒

*Asking a working writer what he thinks about
critics is like asking a lamp-post what he feels about dogs.*
—John Osborne,
English actor, playwright & screenwriter (1929–1994)

⌒‿⌒

*From time to time it's nice to have a book
you can hate—it clears the pipes.*
—Peter Prescott,
American author and book critic (1935–2004).

⌒‿⌒

*When the critic has said everything in his power
about a literary text, he has still said nothing; for the
very existence of literature implies that it cannot be
replaced by non-literature.*
—Tzvetan Todorov,
Bulgarian-French historian, philosopher & essayist
(1939–2017)

⌒‿⌒

*I found the Second Symphony of Sibelius vulgar,
self-indulgent, and provincial beyond all description.*
—Virgil Thomson,
New York Herald Tribune 1940

⌒‿⌒

A statue has never been set up in honour of a critic!
—**Jean Sibelius,**
Finnish composer & violinist (1865–1957)

If you go up high, then use your own leg!
Do not get yourself carried aloft;
do not seat yourself on other peoples backs and heads.
—**Friedrich Nietzsche,**
German Philosopher (1844–1900)

Criticism is the art wherewith a critic tries
to guess himself into a share of the artist's fame.
—**George Jean Nathan,**
American drama critic (1882–1958)

I have long felt that any reviewer who expresses rage
and loathing for a novel is preposterous. He or she
is like a person who has just put on full armor and
attacked a hot fudge sundae or banana split.
—**Kurt Vonnegut, Jr.,**
American writer (1922–2007).

Henry Fielding's **Tom Jones**... *A book intended to sap the foundation of that morality which it is the duty of parents and all public instructors to inculcate in the minds of young people.*
—**Sir John Hawkins**,
English magistrate, writer and biographer
of the life of Samuel Johnson (1719–1789)

I can assure the American public that the errors in **Johnson's Dictionary** *(Samuel Johnson) are ten times as numerous as they suppose; and the confidence now reposed in its accuracy is the greatest injury to philology that now exists.*
—**Noah Webster**,
American lexicographer

I never desire to converse with a man who has written more than he has read.
—**Samuel Johnson** (referred to as Dr. Johnson)
English writer, poet, essayist, moralist, literary critic,
biographer, editor and lexicographer (1709–1784).

*D.H. Lawrence has a diseased mind (***Lady Chatterly's Lover***). He is obsessed by sex...we have no doubt that he will be ostracized by all except the most degenerate coteries in the literary world.*
—**John Bull** (Sunday newspaper established in London)

It *(William Shakespeare's* **Hamlet***) is a vulgar and barbarous drama, which would not be tolerated by the vilest populace of France, or Italy.*
—Voltaire,
French Enlightenment writer & philosopher (1694–1778)

Shakespeare's **Midsummer Night's Dream**...
*The most insipid, ridiculous play
that I ever saw in my life.*
—Samuel Pepys,
Member of English Parliament, famous for his diary
(1633–1703)

*A fool thinks himself to be wise,
but a wise man knows himself to be a fool.*
—William Shakespeare,
England's national poet & the "Bard of Avon" (1564 –1616).

*Ralph Waldo Emerson...
A hoary-headed and toothless baboon.*
—Thomas Carlyle,
Scottish philosopher & satirical writer (1795–1881)

Critics in New York are made by their dislikes,
not by their enthusiasm.
—Irwin Shaw,
American playwright, screenwriter & novelist (1913–1984)

Reviewers are usually people who would have been
poets, historians, biographers etc., if they could; they
have tried their talents at one time or another, and
have failed; therefore they turn critics.
—Samuel Taylor Coleridge,
English poet, literary critic & philosopher (1772–1834)

Tchaikovsky's First Piano Concerto,
like the first pancake, is a flop.
—Nicolai Soloviev,
Russian composer (1846–1916)

Where the heart does not enter; there can be no music.
—Pyotr Ilyich Tchaikovsky,
Russian Composer (1840–1893)

It's those damn critics again.
—Irwin Shaw,
American playwright, screenwriter & novelist (1913–1984)

How trite and feeble and conventional the tunes are; so derivative, so stale, so inexpressive!

Lawrence Gilman on Gershwin's "Rhapsody in Blue."

Lolita, light of my life, fire of my loins. My sin, my soul.

Vladimir Nabokov, "Lolita"

I got rhythm, I got music....Who could ask for anything more?

George Gershwin, "Girl Crazy"

Hands off my score! That's my advice to you, Sir, or to hell with you!

Richard Wagner, in a letter to a teacher

"An American in Paris" is nauseous claptrap, so dull, patchy, thin, vulgar, long-winded and inane.

H.F. Peyser on

Any bookseller should be very sure that he knows in advance that he is selling very literate pornography.

"Kirkus Reviews," (1958) on Nabokov's

Is Wagner a human being at all? Is he not rather a disease? ... He has made music sick.

Friedrich Nietzsche, "Der Fall Wagner"

For critics I care the five hundredth part of the tythe of a half-farthing.
Charles Lamb,
English essayist &
humorist

Picasso enjoys making repulsive works out of beautiful subjects.
Raymond Mortimer,
"Try anything Once"

I paint objects as I think them, not as I see them.
Pablo Picasso,
Spanish artist

Charles Lamb I sincerely believe to be in some considerable degree insane.
Thomas Carlyle,
Scottish essayist

Tell me, how did you love my picture?
Samuel Goldwyn,
MGM movie mogul

The film suffers under its own weight and becomes tedious and heavy.
"Rating the Movies," on
MGM's "The Good Earth"

Winston would go up to his
Creator and say that he
would very much like to meet
His Son, about whom he had
heard a great deal....
David Lloyd George, "Diary"

Attila the Hen
*Clement Freud on
Margaret Thatcher*

In politics, if you want
anything said, ask a man;
if you want anything done,
ask a woman.
*Margaret Thatcher, British
Prime Minister 1979-1990*

She is trying to wear
the trousers of
Winston Churchill.
*Leonid Breshnev on
Margaret Thatcher*

She is the best
man in England.
*Ronald Reagan on
Margaret Thatcher*

We are all worms, but
I do believe I am a
glow worm.
*Winston Churchill,
British statesman*

If you must deal in
criticism, confine your
practice to self-criticism
*"The Little Red Book of
Alcoholics Anonymous"*

. Beethoven's one hundred and thirty-fifth work...gives evidence of an unbalanced mind.
"American Art Journal," 1866

Advise your reviewers to be more circumspect and intelligent.... Your reviewers outcry against me was at first very mortifying.
Ludvig van Beethoven, in a letter to Breitkopf & Hartel

As a writer he has mastered everything except language...as an artist he is everything except articulate.
Oscar Wilde, on George Meredith

God tells me how he want his music played—and you get in His way.
Arturo Toscanini Italian conductor

No passion in the world is equal to the passion to alter someone else's draft.
H.G. Wells, British novelist & historian

What a tiresome affected sod.
Noel Coward, on Oscar Wilde

The critic leaves at curtain fall
To find, in starting to review it,
He scarcely saw the play at all
For watching his reaction to it.
E.B. White, American author & humorist

To escape criticism—
do nothing, say nothing,
be nothing.

Elbert Hubbard, Ameri-
can author & publisher

I like only destructive
critics, because they force
me to...readjust my ideas.

Peter Ustinov,
British writer and actor

Can't a critic give his
opinion of an omelette
without being asked to
lay an egg?

Clayton Rawson, "No
Coffin for the
Corpse"

The temptation is tremendous
to say that you like what you
think you ought to like and
don't like what you think you
oughtn't to like.

Arnold Bennett, British
playright & journalist

In the arts, the critic is
the only independent
source of information.
The rest is advertising.

Pauline Kael, film critic

Comedy is criticism.

Louis Kronenberger
"The Thread of
Laughter"

It takes a rare person
to want to hear what he
doesn't want to hear.

Dick Cavett, American
talk show host

*Look, failure is inevitable for the writer. Any writer.
I don't care who he is, or how great he is, or what
he's written. Sooner or later he's going to flop and
everybody who admired him will try to write him off
as a bum.*
    —**Michael Beahan Shnayerson**,
American journalist and biographer of Irwin Shaw

*I cringe when critics say I'm a master
of the popular novel. What's an unpopular novel?*
    —**Irwin Shaw**,
American playwright, screenwriter & novelist (1913–1984)

*I played over the music of that scoundrel Brahms.
What a giftless bastard! It annoys me that this
self-inflated mediocrity is hailed as a genius.*
    —**Pyotr Ilyich Tchaikovsky**,
Russian Composer (1840–1893)

*If there is anyone here whom I have not insulted,
I beg his pardon.*
    —**Johannes Brahms**,
German composer (1833–1897)

Every rule in the realm of traditional music writing was broken by Prokofiev. Dissonance followed dissonance in a fashion inconceivable to ears accustomed to melody and harmonic laws upon which their musical comprehension has been reared.
—**New York Sun** 1918

The time has past when music was written for a handful of aesthetes.
—**Sergey Prokofiev**
(Sergey Sergeyevich Prokofiev) Russian composer (1891- 1953)

Prokofiev blazed new trails with is work, opening up horizons for modern music.
—**Emile Gilels,**
Russian pianist. (1916–1985)

Critics sometimes appear to be addressing themselves to works other than those I remember writing.
—**Joyce Carol Oates,**
American writer (1938–)

For God's sake (I was never more serious)
don't make me ridiculous any more by
terming me gentle-hearted in print.
—Charles Lamb,
English poet & antiquarian (1775–1834)

Keep away from people who belittle your ambitions.
Small people always do that, but the really great
make you feel that you too, can become great.
—Mark Twain,
American writer & humorist (1835–1910)

An evil person is like a dirty window;
they never let the light shine through.
—William Makepeace Thackeray,
English writer (1811–1863)

Why did all the giants descend on me and my little
stories? I wasn't doing anything of national import.
All I was trying to do was entertain the public and
make a buck.
—Mickey Spillane,
American crime novelist (1918–2006)

Part 4.

Observations & Penguinations
CELEBRATING FRESHNESS OF VISION

Joy
Enthusiasm
Optimism
Attitude
Positivity
Passion

*If you hear a voice within you say 'you cannot paint,'
then by all means paint and that voice will be silenced.*
—**Vincent van Gogh**,
Dutch Post-Impressionist painter (1853–1890)

*All the sorrows, all the bitterness, all the sadnesses,
I forget them and ignore them in the joy of working.*
—**Camille Pissarro**,
Danish-French artist (1830–1903)

*What we perceive and understand
depends upon what we are.*
—**Aldous Huxley**,
English writer & philosopher (1894–1963)

*Happiness is not achieved by
the conscious pursuit of happiness;
it is generally the by-product of other activities.*
—**Aldous Huxley**,
English writer & philosopher (1894–1963)

Yesterday the sun went hence,
And yet it is here today.
—**John Donne**,
Poet, priest, lawyer (1573–1633)

Tomorrow to fresh woods and pastures new.
—**John Milton,**
English poet (1608–1674)

In the realm of ideas everything depends on enthusiasm.
—**Goethe,**
German writer (1749–1832)

Exuberance is Beauty
—**William Blake**,
English poet & painter (1757–1827)

Everybody has a creative potential and from the moment
you can express this…you can start to change the world.
—**Paulo Coelho,**
Brazilian lyricist & novelist (1947–)

You're never too old to set another goal
or to dream a new dream.
—C.S. Lewis,
British novelist & poet (1898–1963)

⌒⌒

The only way to discover the limits of the possible
is to go beyond them into the impossible.
—Arthur C. Clarke,
British science fiction writer (1917–2008)

⌒⌒

Very little is needed to make a happy life;
It is all within yourself, in your way of thinking.
—Marcus Aurelius,
Roman Emperor (161–180)

⌒⌒

The quality of your life depends
on the quality of your thoughts.
—Marcus Aurelius,
Roman Emperor (161–180)

⌒⌒

If you don't like something, change it.
If you can't change it, change yourself.
—Maya Angelou,
American writer (1928–2014)

When we are no longer able to change a situation—
we are challenged to change ourselves.
—Viktor E. Frankl,
Philosopher, Holocaust survivor (1905–1997)

Don't cry because it's over, smile because it happened.
—Dr. Seuss *(Theodor Seuss Geisel)*
an American writer & cartoonist (1904–1991)

The worst sin—perhaps the only sin—
passion can commit is to be joyless.
—Dorothy Sayers,
British novelist and playwright ((1893–1957)

An optimist is a person who sees a green light everywhere.
—Albert Schweitzer,
humanitarian physician (1875–1965)

The mind acts like an enemy
for those who do not control it.
—Bhagavad Gita,
Hindu Scripture (5th–2nd Century BCE)

Got no check books, got no banks,
Still I'd like to express my thanks—
I got the sun in the mornin'
And the moon at night.
—**Irvin Berlin**
(1888–1989) "I Got the Sun in the Morning" (song)

If opportunity doesn't knock, build a door.
—**Milton Berle,**
American comedian and actor. (1908–2002)

Happiness never decreases by being shared
—**Buddha**

The smile is the shortest distance between two persons.
—**Victor Borge,**
pianist, conductor, comedian, (1909–2000)

We first make our habits, then our habits make us.
—**John Dryden,**
England's first Poet Laureate (1631–1700)

*"Keep your thoughts positive
because your thoughts become your words.*

*Keep your words positive
because your words become your behavior.*

*Keep your behavior positive
because your behavior becomes your habits.*

*Keep your habits positive
because your habits become your values.*

*Keep your values positive
because your values become your destiny."*
—Mahatma Gandhi,
Indian Nationalist and Spiritual leader (1869-**1948)**

They can because they think they can.
—Virgil,
Ancient Roman poet (70 BC–19 BC)

The happiest of all lives is a busy solitude.
—Voltaire,
Enlightenment writer (1694–1778)

I came near to ending my own life—
only art held me back.
—Ludwig van Beethoven
(1770–1827) German-born musical genius

———~·~———

There is more to life than increasing its speed.
—Mahatma Gandhi,
Indian Nationalist and Spiritual leader (1869–**1948)**

———~·~———

Man's mind, once stretched by a new idea,
never regains its original dimensions.
—Oliver Wendell Holmes Jr.,
U.S. Supreme Court Justice (1841–1935)

———~·~———

Many persons have the wrong idea of what constitutes
true happiness. It is not attained through self-
gratification but through fidelity to a worthy purpose.
—Helen Keller,
American author & activist (1880–1968)

———~·~———

Happy accidents are real gifts, and they can
open the door to a future that didn't even exist.
—David Lynch,
American artist and film director, (1946–)

Happy days are here again,
the skies above are clear again…
—Jack Yellen,
American lyricist (1892–1991)

Luck is believing you're lucky.
—**Tennessee Williams**,
American playwright (1911–1983)

"The man who makes everything that leads to
happiness depend upon himself, and not upon other
men, has adopted the very best plan for living happily."
—**Plato**,
philosopher in Classical Greece
(428/427 BC–348/347 BC)

We can easily forgive a child who is afraid of the dark.
The real tragedy of life is when men are afraid of the light.
—**Plato**,
philosopher in Classical Greece
(428/427 BC–348/347 BC)

An unfulfilled vocation drains the color
from a man's entire existence.
—Honoré de Balzac,
French writer (1799–1850)

He that leaveth nothing to
Chance will do few things Ill,
but will do few things.
—George Halifax,
English statesman (1633–1695)

Without feeling, whatever you do amounts to nothing.
—Billie Holiday,
American born jazz singer (1915–1959)

A musician must make music,
An artist must paint, a poet must write
if he is to be ultimately at peace with himself.
—Abraham Maslow,
American psychologist (1908–1970)

The passion of the artist is humble.
He is essentially a channel.
—**Piet Mondrian**,
Dutch artist (1872–1944)

Color is my day-long obsession, joy and torment.
—**Claude Monet**,
French artist (1840–1926)

The only thing more tormenting
than writing is not writing.
—**Cynthia Ozick**,
American novelist (1928–)

I found I could say things with color and shapes
that I couldn't say in any other way—
things that I had no words for.
—**Georgia O' Keefe**,
American artist (1888–1976)

Color is one of the great things in the world
that makes it worth living for me…
(I) paint color for the world—life as I see it.
—Georgia O' Keefe,
American artist (1888–1976)

The greater danger for all of us lies not in setting our
aims too high and falling short; but in setting our
aims to low, and achieving our mark.
—Michelangelo,
Italian sculptor and painter (1475–1564)

Sooner or later I'm going to die,
but I'm not going to retire.
—Margaret Mead,
American anthropologist (1901–1978)

The essence of all art is to have
pleasure in giving pleasure.
—Mikhail Baryshnikov,
Russian ballet dancer & actor (1948–)

My work is loving the world,
Here the sunflowers, there the hummingbird…
Equal seekers of sweetness.
—Mary Oliver,
American poet (1935–)

~~~

Writing isn't a game to me…
Neither is it 'a job'. It is my life…
it enrages me to see people playing at being a writer.
—Harlan Ellison,
American writer (1934–)

~~~

The one important thing I have learned over the years
is the difference between taking one's work seriously
and taking one's self seriously. The first is imperative
and the second is disastrous.
—Margot Fonteyn,
ballerina with Royal Ballet (1919–1991)

~~~

We must be willing to let go of the life we have planned,
so as to have the life that is waiting for us.
—E.M. Forster,
English writer (1879–1970)

~~~

I can't understand how anyone is able to paint without optimism. Despite the general pessimistic attitude in the world today, I am nothing but an optimist.
—**Hans Hoffman**,
painter (1880–1966)

Enthusiasm is a great hill-climber.
—**Elbert Hubbard**,
philosopher, artist (1865–1915)

Opportunities are usually disguised as hard work, so most people don't recognize them.
—**Anna Landers**,
American advice columnist (1918–2002)

Our aspirations are our possibilities.
—**Robert Browning**,
English poet (1812–1889)

I love making movies.
If I wasn't paid to do it, I would pay to do it.
—**David Lean**,
English film director (1908–1991)

Part 5.

Observations & Penguinations
MERRYMAKING WITH
FRESHNESS OF VISION

Humor
Connectivity
Possibility
Trust
Abundance

All higher humor begins with
ceasing to take oneself seriously.
—Hermann Hesse,
writer & painter (1877–1962)

———~——

A man may pretend to be serious;
he cannot pretend to be witty.
—Sacha Guitry,
French actor & writer (1885–1957).

———~——

All the wit in the world is lost
upon him who has none.
—La Bruyère,
French philosopher & satirist (1645- 1696)

———~——

A humorist is no more an expert on humor than a
man suffering from diabetes is an 'expert' on diabetes.
He—like the diabetic—has got it, but he has no idea
how he got it and still less how to get rid of it.
—George Mikes,
Hungarian-born British humorist and writer (1912–1987)

———~——

From there to here and here to there,
Funny things are everywhere.
One fish, Two fish, Red Fish, Blue Fish,
—Dr. Seuss (Theodor Seuss Geisel)
an American writer and cartoonist (1904–1991)

I just draw what I think or what I hope will be funny
things. If people read more into them, that's fine.
—Charles M. Schultz,
American cartoonist (1922–2000)

Laughter is sunshine;
it chases winter from the human face.
—Victor Hugo,
French writer (1802–1885)

Some combinations are important and some are trivial…
a person who cannot tell them apart must labor
under a terrible disadvantage.
—Isaac Asimov,
Science writer & biochemist (1920–1992)

*The only reason for being a professional writer
is that you just can't help it.*
—Leo Rosten,
American humorist (1908–1997)

*Why do you sit there and look like an envelope
without any address on it.*
—Mark Twain,
writer & humorist (1835–1910)

*The art of Biography Is different from Geography,
Geography is about maps,
But Biography is about chaps.*
—Edmund Clerihew Bentley,
English novelist (1875–1956)

*The difference between the right word and the almost
right word is the difference between lightning and a
lightning bug.*
—Mark Twain,
writer & humorist (1835–1910)

*I am trying to cultivate a life-style
that does not require my presence.*
—Gary Trudeau,
American cartoonist (1948–)

I'm not funny. What I am is brave.
—Lucille Ball,
American actor & comedian (1911–1989)

*Once, my spirit went to Miami for a weekend, and
once it was arrested for trying to leave Macy's without
paying for a tie. The fourth time, it was actually my
body that left my spirit.*
—Woody Allen,
American writer & filmmaker (1935–)

*The concept of absurdity is something
I am attracted to.*
—David Lynch,
American film director & producer (1946–)

Be yourself; everyone else is already taken.
—Oscar Wilde,
Irish poet & playwright (1854–1900)

Consistency is the last refuge of the unimaginative.
—Oscar Wilde,
Irish poet & playwright (1854–1900)

The smile is the shortest distance between two persons.
—Victor Borge,
pianist, conductor, comedian, (1909–2000)

If you wish in this world to advance,
Your merits you're bound to enhance;
You must stir it and stump it
And blow your own trumpet,
Or trust me, you haven't a chance.
—William Schwenck Gilbert,
librettist (1836–1911)

Adam was the only man who, when he said a good thing,
knew that nobody had said it before him.
—Mark Twain,
American writer & humorist (1835–1910)

There is nothing funnier than the human animal.
—Walt Disney,
pioneer of the American animation industry (1901–1966)

*I am a writer who keeps seeing things
in terms of funny things.*
—Charles M. Schultz,
American cartoonist (1922–2000)

Comedy is simply a funny way of being serious.
—Peter Ustinov,
British writer & actor, (1921–2004)

One can't be angry when one looks at a penguin.
—John Ruskin,
English art critic (1819–1900)

*As drunks, the angry penguins of the night,
straddling the cobbles of the square,
tying a shoelace by fogged lamplight.*
—Max Harris,
Mithridatum of Despair Australian poet and writer

If I could come back as anything—
I'd be a bird, first.
—Nikki Giovanni,
writer (1943–)

⁓

Ford...you're turning into a penguin. Stop it.
—Douglas Adams,
English writer *Hitchhiker's Guide to the Galaxy* (1952–2001)

Part 6.

Observations & Penguinations
ONWARDS WITH FRESHNESS OF VISION

Purpose
Commitment
Persistence
Decision
Grit
The Long Haul

Great minds have purposes, others have wishes.
—Washington Irving,
writer and statesman, 1783–1859)

⌒‿⌒

Looking back, my life seems like one long obstacle race,
with me as chief obstacle.
—Jack Paar,
American author & TV host (1918–2004)

⌒‿⌒

We know what happens to people
who stay in the middle of the road. They get run over.
—Aneurin Bevan,
Welsh politician ((1897–1960)

⌒‿⌒

If the creator had a purpose in equipping us with a neck,
he certainly meant for us to stick it out.
—Arthur Koestler,
Hungarian-born English author (1905–1983)

⌒‿⌒

You've got to get up every morning with determination
to be able to go to bed with satisfaction.
—George Horace Lorimer,
American journalist and author (1867–1937)

He slept beneath the moon,
he basked beneath the sun;
he lived a life of going-to-do,
and died with nothing done.
—**James Albery**,
British playwright (1838–1889)

Action is the foundational key to all success.
—**Pablo Picasso**,
Spanish artist (1881–1973)

Let me tell you the secret that led to my goal.
My strength lies solely in my tenacity.
—**Louis Pasteur**,
French microbiologist & chemist (1822–1895)

Only put off until tomorrow what
you are willing to die having left undone.
—**Pablo Picasso**,
Spanish artist (1881–1973)

If my doctor told me I had only six minutes to live,
I wouldn't brood. I'd type a little faster.
   —**Isaac Asimov**,
   Science writer & biochemist (1920–1992)

Far away there in the sunshine are my highest
aspirations. I may not reach them, but I can look
up and see their beauty, believe in them, and try to
follow where they lead.
   —**Louisa May Alcott**,
   American novelist & poet (1832–1888)

Our aspirations are our possibilities.
   —**Robert Browning**,
   English poet (1812–1889)

The man who can drive himself further once
the effort gets painful is the man who will win.
   —**Roger Bannister**,
   English athlete, record-breaking runner ((1929–)

Many of life's failures are people who did not realize how close they were to success when they gave up.
—Thomas A. Edison,
inventor (1847–1931)

The value of an idea lies in the using of it.
—Thomas A. Edison,
inventor (1847–1931)

The only person you are destined to become is the person you decide to be.
—Ralph Waldo Emerson,
American poet & essayist (1803–1882)

Good thoughts are no better than dreams, unless they be executed!
—Ralph Waldo Emerson,
American poet & essayist (1803–1882)

Everything in the universe goes by indirection. There are no straight lines.
—Ralph Waldo Emerson,
American poet & essayist (1803–1882)

Not enjoyment, and not sorrow,
Is our destined end or way;
But to act, that each tomorrow
Finds us further than today.
—Henry Wadsworth Longfellow*,*
American poet (1807–1882)

How can I know what I think till I see what I say?
—E.M. Forster,
English writer (1879–1970)

If at first you don't succeed, try, try again.
Then quit. No use being a damn fool about it.
—W.C. Fields.
American comedian & writer (1880–1946)

He that would thrive
Must rise at five.
He that hath thriven
May lie still till seven.
—John Clarke,
writer (1609–1676)

The person who makes a success of living is the one who
sees his goal steadily and aims for it unswervingly.
—Cecil B. DeMille,
American Filmmaker (1881–1959)

The secret of getting things done is to act!
—Dante,
Italian Renaissance poet (1265–1321)

The time for action is now.
It's never too late to do something.
—De Saint-Exupéry,
French writer, poet, aristocrat, journalist,
and pioneering aviator. (1900–1944)

The secret of success is constancy to purpose.
—Benjamin Disraeli,
British statesman (1804–1881)

I think;
Therefore I am.
Cogito, Ergo Sum.
—René Descartes,
French philosopher, mathematician, and scientist (1596–1650)

*You can never cross the ocean unless
you have the courage to lose sight of the shore.*
—**Andrè Gide**,
French writer & Nobel Laureate (1869–1951)

*I know of no more encouraging fact than the
unquestionable ability of man to elevate his life by a
conscious endeavor."*
—**Henry David Thoreau**,
American writer & poet (1817–1862)

*A writer who waits for ideal conditions under which to
work will die without putting a word on paper.*
—**E.B. White**,
American writer (1899–1985)

Ultimately, my hope is to amaze myself.
—**Jerry Uelsmann**,
American photographer (1934–)

Great works are performed not by strength
but by perseverance.
—**Samuel Johnson**,
writer & lexicographer (1709–1784)

Life is brief, art is long.
—**Hippocrates**,
Greek physician (460–370 BC)

A ship in harbor is safe,
but that is not what ships are built for.
—**John A. Shedd**,
American writer (1859–1928)

Take something.
Do something to it,
Do something else on it.
—**Jasper Johns**,
American artist (1930–)

As one gets older one sees more paths that could be
taken. Artists sense within their own work that kind

of swelling of possibilities which may seem a freedom
or a confusion.
—Jasper Johns,
American artist (1930–)

Nothing else in the world…not all the armies…
is so powerful as an idea whose time has come.
—Victor Hugo,
French writer (1802–1885)

We shall not cease from exploration
And the end of all our exploring
Will be where we started
And know the place for the first time.
—T.S. Eliot,
British poet & playwright (1888–1965)

We mustn't stop now or well be late.
Late for what? For what we want to be in time for.
—A.A. Milne
The House at Pooh Corner, English writer (1882–1956)

It is good to have an end to journey toward:
but it is the journey that matters in the end.
—Ursula K. Le Guin,
American writer (1929–)

Long is the road from conception to completion.
—Molière,
French playwright & actor (1622 –1673)

Quotation Biographies

A

Abrahams—*Lionel Abrahams, South African novelist, poet, editor, critic, essayist & publisher (1928–2004).*

Achebe—*Chinua Achebe, Nigerian novelist, poet, critic and professor (1930–2013).*

Adams—Ansel Adams, *American photographer and environmentalist (1924–2007).*

Adams—*Douglas Adams (Douglas Noel Adams) English writer, scriptwriter & dramatist—Hitchhiker's Guide to the Galaxy—(1952–2001)*

Adams—*John Quincy Adams, American statesman, diplomat, ambassador and United States Senator (1767–1848).*

Adams—Scott Adams, *American cartoonist and author (1957–).*

Albee—*Edward Albee, Pulitzer Prize-winning American playwright (1928–2016).*

Albers—*Josef Albers, German-born artist and educator instrumental in bringing the Weimer Germany Art School style (Bauhaus) to America. (1888–1976).*

Albery—*James Albery, British playwright (1838–1889).*

Alcott—*Louisa May Alcott, American novelist and poet (1832–1888).*

Alexander—*Lloyd Alexander (Lloyd Chudley) American Author primarily of fantasy novels for children and adults (1924–2007).*

Allen—*Woody Allen, (Allan Stewart Konigsberg) American film-maker, writer, actor, comedian (1935–).*

American Art Journal, *1866*

Angelou—*Maya Angelou (Marguerite Johnson) American poet, storyteller, civil rights activist and autobiographer (1928–2014).*

Asimov—*Isaac Asimov, Russian-born American biochemist Science writer of over 500 books (1920–1992).*

Aurelius—*Marcus Aurelius, Roman emperor (161–180).*

B

Babailov—*Igor Babailov Igor (Valerievich Babailov) Russian-born American painter and portrait artist (1965–)*

Bacon—*Francis Bacon, Irish-born British painter (1909–1992)*

Ball—*Lucille Ball (Lucille Désirée Ball Morton) American actor, comedian, film-studio executive, and producer. Star of the self-produced sitcoms such as (1911–1989)*

Balzac—*Honoré de Balzac, French novelist & playwright (1799–1850)*

Bannister—*Roger Bannister (Sir) English athlete, physician, academic and the first person to run a mile in under 4 minutes (1929–2018)*

Baruch—*Bernard Mannes Baruch, American financier, philanthropist and statesman (1870–1965).*

Baryshnikov—*Mikhail Baryshnikov, Russian dancer and actor, started with the Kirov Ballet in Leningrad, joined City Ballet—one of the greatest dancers of all time. (1948–)*

Baudelaire—*Charles Pierre Baudelaire, 19ᵗʰ Century French poet, essayist and translator of Edgar Allan Poe (1861–1867)*

Baziotes—*William Baziotes, American painter influenced by Surrealism. A contributor to Abstract Expressionism (1912–1963)*

Beethoven—*Ludvig van Beethoven, German composer & pianist (1770–1827)*

Bell—*Alexander Graham Bell, Scottish-born American scientist and inventor who patented the first practical telephone (1877–1922)*

Bellow—*(Solomom Bellows) Canadian-American author, winner of a Pulitzer and the 1976 Nobel Prize for literature (1915–2005)*

Bennett—*Arnold Bennet, British playwright & journalist (1867–1931)*

Bentley—*Edmund Clerihew Bentley, English novelist, humorist and inventor of Clerihew Verse (1875–1956).*

Berle—*Milton Berle (Mendel Berlinger) American comedian and actor. (1908–2002)*

Berlin—*Irving Berlin (Israel Bailin) Russian-born American composer and lyricist (1888–1989).*

Bevan—*Aneurin Bevan, Welsh politician (1897 -1960)*

Bhagavad Gita—*700 verse Hindu scripture in Sanskrit (thought to be from 5ᵗʰ Century to 2ⁿᵈ Century BCE).*

Billings—*Josh Billings (Henry Wheeler Shaw), American writer and humorist (1818–1885).*

Blake—*William Blake, English poet, painter, and printmaker. (1757–1827)*

Bleecher—*Henry Ward Bleecher, American clergyman (1813–1887)*

Bodhidharma—*Bodhidharma, also known as Daruma in Japan, was an Indian Buddhist monk, who is commonly considered the founder of Chan Buddhism in China (450-500 A.D).*

Borge—*Victor Borge (Børge Rosenbaum) (1909–2000), Danish and American comedian, conductor, and pianist who blended music and comedy (1909–2000)*

Bradbury—*Ray Bradbury (Ray Douglas Bradbury), American literary author of highly imaginative short stories and novels, (1920–2012).*

Brahms—*Johannes Brahms German composer & pianist (1833–1897.*

Brancusi—*Constantine Brancusi, Romanian sculptor, painter and photographer, a pioneer of modernism who lived and worked in France (1976–1957)*

Braque—*Georges Braque, French Painter, Collagist, Draftsman, Printmaker and Sculptor major in the Cubism Movement (1882–1963)*

Brenan—*Gerald Brenan (Edward FitzGerald) British writer who wrote largely about Spain. (1894–1987)*

Breton—*André Breton, French poet & founder of Surrealism (1896–1966)*

Breshnev—*Leonid Ilyich Breshnev, General Secretary of the Central Committee of the Communist Party of the Soviet Union (1906–1982)*

Browning -*Robert Browning, English poet (1812–1889)*

Buddha

Bull—*John Bull (Sunday newspaper established in London).*

Burroughs—*William Burroughs, American writer, artist and important Beat Generation figure (1914–1997)*

C

Capote—*Truman Capote, American novelist, short story and non-fiction writer, screenwriter, playwright (1924–1984)*

Capra—*Frank Capra (Francesco Rosario Capra) Italian-born American film director, writer & producer (1897–1991).*

Carlyle—*Thomas Carlyle, Scottish philosopher, satirical writer, essayist, translator, historian, mathematician, and teacher (1795–1881)*

Carroll—*Lewis Carroll (Charles Lutwidge Dodgson) English writer, mathematician, logician, Anglican deacon, and photographer (1832–1898)*

Cavett—*Dick Cavett, American television personality & talk show host (1936–)*

Chagall—*Marc Chagall, Belarus-born French painter, printmaker, and designer of emotionally poetic art. (1887–1985)*

Chandler—*Raymond Chandler (Raymond Thornton Chandler) American novelist of mainly detective fiction, and a screenwriter (1888–1959)*

Cheever—*John Cheever, American novelist and short story writer. (1912–1982)*

Chinese proverbial wisdom

Chinese proverb

Churchill—*Winston Churchill, British statesman, army officer, writer & Prime Minister of the United Kingdom (1874–1965)*

Clancy—*Tom Clancy (Thomas Leo Clancy Jr.) American novelist largely of espionage and military-sciences set during and after the Cold War. (1947–2013)*

Clarke—*Sir Arthur Charles Clarke, CBE, FRAS was a British science fiction writer, science writer and futurist, inventor, undersea explorer, and television series host (1917–2008)*

Clarke—*John Clarke, 17th century writer (1609–1676)*

Cocteau—*Jean Cocteau, French writer, artist, filmmaker (1889–1963)*

Coelho—*Paulo Coelho de Souza is a Brazilian lyricist and novelist (1947–)*

Coleridge—*Samuel Taylor Coleridge, English poet, literary critic, philosopher and theologian. He and William Wordsworth, were founders of the Romantic Movement in England (1772–1834)*

Copland—*Aaron Copland, American composer of distinctive American musical themes (1900–1990)*

Cousteau—*Jacques Yves Cousteau AC, French naval officer, explorer, conservationist, filmmaker, scientist, photographer, studied the sea and life in water (1910–1997)*

Coward—*Noel Coward (Sir Noel Pierce Coward) English playwright, composer, actor & singer (1899–1973)*

Coypel—*Antoine Coypel, French painter (1661–1722)*

D

Dante—*Dante (Durante degli Alighieri), major Italian poet of the Late Middle Ages/Early Renaissance. (1265–1321)*

Daumal—*Renee Daumal, French spiritual writer & poet (1908–1944)*

Da Vinci—*Leonardo Da Vinci (Leonardo di ser Piero da Vinci) Italian Renaissance inventor, painter, sculptor, interested also in science, astronomy, anatomy, architecture, writing, etc. (1452–1519)*

Debussy—*Claude Debussy, French composer (1862–1918)*

De Châteaubriand—*François-Rene de Châteaubriand, French writer (1768–1848)*

Degas—*Edgar Degas, French painter and sculptor (1834–1917)*

Delacroix—*Eugène Delacroix—(Ferdinand Victor Eugène Delacroix) French artist of the French Romantic school. (1796/98–1863)*

De Lilo—*Don De Lilo, American novelist & playwright (1936–)*

de Mille—*Agnes de Mille, American dancer and Choreographer (1905–1993)*

DeMille—*Cecil B. DeMille (Cecil Blount DeMille) American film-maker—silent and sound (1881–1959)*

Demuth—*Charles Demuth, (Charles Henry Buckius Demuth) American watercolorist who turned to oils late in his career, developing a style of painting known as Precisionism (1883–1935)*

De Saint-Exupéry—*De Saint-Exupéry (Antoine Marie Jean-Baptiste Roger, comte de Saint-Exupéry) French writer, poet, journalist, & pioneering aviator (1900–1944)*

De San Concordio—*Bartolommeo De San Concordio, Florentine painter & writer (1260–1347)*

Descartes—*René Descartes, French philosopher, mathematician, and scientist (1596–1650)*

Dillard—*R.H.W. Dillard (Richard Henry Wilde Dillard) American poet, author, critic, and translator. (1937–)*

Disney—*Walt Disney, entrepreneur & pioneer of the American animation industry (1901–1966)*

Disraeli—*Benjamin Disraeli Disraeli, 1st Earl of Beaconsfield, KG, PC, FRS was a British statesman of the Conservative Party who twice served as Prime Minister of the United Kingdom. (1804–1881)*

Doctorow—*E.L. Doctorow (Edgar Lawrence) American novelist, editor, and professor (1931–2015)*

Donne—*John Donne, poet, priest, lawyer (1573–1633)*

Dryden—*John Dryden English poet, critic & playwright and England's first Poet Laureate (1631–1700)*

Duchamp—*Marcel Duchamp (Henri-Robert-Marcel Duchamp) French-American painter of Cubism, Conceptual Art, and Dada, sculptor, chess player and writer (1887–1968)*

E

Edison—*Thomas Edison (Thomas Alva Edison), American inventor who, singly or jointly, held a world record 1,093 patents. (1847–1931)*

Einstein—*Albert Einstein, German-born theoretical physicist, philosopher and Nobel Laureate who developed the theory of relativity. (1879–1955)*

Eliot—*T.S. Eliot (Thomas Stearns Eliot, OM) British essayist, poet, publisher, playwright, literary and social critic (1888–1965)*

Ellison—*Harlan Ellison (Harlan Jay Ellison) American writer of mainly speculative fiction (short stories, novellas, screenplays, comic book scripts, teleplays, essays, screen plays, comic book scripts etc.) (1934–)*

Emerson—*Ralph Waldo Emerson, American essayist & poet and leader of the transcendentalist movement (1803–1882*

Epstein—*Jacob Epstein (Sir Jacob Epstein KBE) American-born British sculptor (1880–1959)*

Escher—*M.C. Escher (Maurits Cornelis Escher) Dutch graphic artist who made mathematically inspired woodcuts, lithographs, and mezzotints (1898–1972*

Evers—*Medgar Evers (Medgar Wiley Evers) American Civil Rights activist in Mississippi (Born 1925–assassinated 1963)*

Evening Standard

F

Fallaci—*Oriana Fallaci, Italian novelist & journalist and political interviewer (1929–2006).*

Feiffer—*Jules Feiffer (Jules Ralph) American syndicated cartoonist and author (1929–)*

Fenton—*James Fenton (James Martin Fenton FRSL FRSA) English poet, journalist and literary critic, (1949–)*

Fields—*W.C. Fields (William Claude Dukenfield) American comedian, actor, juggler and writer (1880–1946)*

Fonteyn—*Margot Fonteyn (Dame Margot Fonteyn de Arias, DBE) English ballerina with the Royal Ballet, appointed Prima Ballerina by Queen Elizabeth II. (1919–1991)*

Forster—*E.M. Forster (Edward Morgan Forster OM CH) English novelist, short story writer, essayist and librettist 1879–1970)*

Frankl—*Viktor E. Frankl, writer, philosopher, neurologist, psychiatrist, Holocaust survivor and founder of logotherapy (1905–1997.*

Freud—*Clement Freud (Sir Clement Raphael Freud) British broadcaster, writer, politician & grandson of Sigmund Freud (1924–2009)*

Freud—*Anna Freud, Austrian-British psychoanalyst, pioneer of child psychoanalysis, youngest child of Sigmund Freud (1895–1982)*

Fromm—*Erich Fromm, (Erich Seligmann Fromm) German social psychologist, psychoanalyst, sociologist, humanistic philosopher, and democratic socialist.(1900–1980).*

Fuentes—*Carlos Fuentes (Carlos Fuentes Macías) Mexican novelist and essayist (1928–2012)*

G

Gaiman—*Neil Gaiman (Neil Richard MacKinnon Gaiman) an English author of short fiction, novels, comic books, graphic novels, audio theatre, and film.(1960–)*

Gandi—*Mahatma Gandi, Hindu Nationalist Leader who led India to independence (1869–1948)*

Gauguin—*Paul Gauguin, French post-impressionist artist (1848–1903)*

George—*David Lloyd George, British statesman (1863–1945)*

Gershwin—*George Gershwin, American composer and pianist (1898–1937)*

Giacometti—*Alberto Giacometti, Swiss sculptor, painter, draughtsman and printmaker (1901 -1966)*

Gibran—*Kahlil Gibran, Lebanese-American poet, artist and philosopher. (1883–1931)*

Gide—*Andrè Gide (Andrè Gide André Paul Guillaume Gide) French author and 1947 winner of the Nobel Prize in Literature (1869–1951)*

Gilbert—*Sir William Schwenck Gilbert, English dramatist, librettist, poet and illustrator also collaborated with the composer Arthur Sullivan (1836–1911)*

Gilels—*Emile Gilels (Emil Grigoryevich Gilels) Soviet pianist (1916–1985)*

Gilman—*Lawrence Gilman, author & music critic (1878–1939)*

Giovanni—*Nikki Giovanni, American poet, writer, activist, and educator (1943)*

Glazer—*Milton Glazer, American artist and graphic designer (1929–)*

Goethe—Goethe *(Johann Wolfgang Von Goethe) German poet, playwright, novelist, scientist, color theorist (1749–1832)*

Golding—*William Golding (Sir William Gerald Golding CBE) British novelist, playwright, and poet. For his novel Lord of the Flies, he won a Nobel Prize in Literature (1911–1993)*

Goldwyn—*Samuel Goldwyn (Samuel Goldfish) MGM movie mogul (1879–1974)*

Graham—*Martha Graham, American modern dancer and choreographer. Her style, the Graham technique, reshaped American dance (1894–1991)*

Guitry—*Sacha Guitry (Alexandre-Pierre Georges) French stage actor, film actor, director, screenwriter, and playwright (1885–1957).*

H

Halifax—*George, Lord Halifax (George Savile, 1st Marquess of Halifax, PC, DL, FRS) English statesman, politician and writer (1633–1695)*

Harris—*Max Harris, Australian poet and writer*

Hawkins—*Sir John Hawkins, English magistrate, writer and biographer of the life of Hawkins—Samuel Johnson (1719–1789)*

Hayakawa—*S.I. Hayakawa, scholar & U.S. senator (1906–1992)*

Hazlett—*William Hazlett, English writer, drama & literary critic, painter, social commentator, and philosopher. (1778–1830)*

Hemingway—*Ernest Hemingway (Ernest Miller Hemingway) American novelist, short story writer, and journalist whose writing style had a strong influence on 20th-century fiction (1899–1961)*

Henri—*Robert Henri, American painter and teacher (1865–1929)*

Heraclitus—*Heraclitus, a Greek philosopher of the late 6th century BCE.*

Hesse—*Hermann Karl Hesse, German-born poet, novelist, and painter. (1877–1962)*

Hippocrates—*Hippocrates, Greek physician of the Age of Pericles, and is considered one of the most outstanding figures in the history of medicine. (460–370 BC)*

Hitchcock—*Alfred Hitchcock (Sir Alfred Joseph Hitchcock KBE) English film director, producer and one of the most influential film-makers in the history of cinema (1899–1980)*

Hoban—*Russell Hoban (Russell Conwell Hoban) American writer who lived in Britain (1925–2011)*

Hoffman—*Hans Hoffman, German-born American abstract expressionist painter (1880–1966)*

Holiday—*Billie Holiday, American born jazz singer (1915–1959)*

Holmes—*Oliver Wendell Holmes Jr., American jurist & from 1930, Acting Chief Justice of the United States (1841–1935)*

Hopper—*Edward Hopper, American realist painter and printmaker (1882–1967)*

Horace—*Horace, (Quintus Horatius Flaccus) Roman, Latin-speaking lyric poet during the time of Augustus. (8, 65 BC–27, 8 BC)*

Hubbard—*Elbert Hubbard, American author & publisher (1856–1915)*

Hugo—*Victor Hugo (Victor Marie Hugo) French poet, novelist, and dramatist of the Romantic movement. (1802–1885)*

Hundertwasser—*Hundertwasser (Friedensreich Regentag Dunkel-bunt) Austrian-born New Zealand artist with architectural sensibilities (1928–2000)*

Huxley—*Aldous Huxley (Aldous Leonard Huxley) English writer, novelist, & philosopher (1894–1963).*

I

Irving—*Washington Irving, American short story writer, essayist, biographer, historian, and statesman (1783–1859)*

J

John Bull *(Sunday newspaper established in London)*

Johns—*Jasper Johns, American painter, sculptor and printmaker associated with Abstract expressionism, Neo-Dada, and Pop art (1930–)*

Johnson—*Samuel Johnson (referred to as Dr. Johnson) English writer, poet, essayist, moralist, literary critic, biographer, editor and lexicographer (1709–1784).*

Joubert—*Joseph Joubert, French moralist and essayist (1754–1824)*

Joyce—*James Joyce (James Augustine Aloysius Joyce) Irish novelist, short story writer, and poet. He contributed to the modernist avant-garde and is regarded as one of the most influential authors of the 20th century (1882–1941)*

Jung—*Carl Jung (Carl Gustav Jung) Swiss psychiatrist and psychoanalyst influential also in anthropology, archaeology, philosophy, literature (1875–1961)*

Juster—*Norton Juster, American academic, architect, and popular writer of books such as* The Phantom Tollbooth and The Dot and the Line. *(1929–)*

K

Kael—*Pauline Kael, American Film Critic (1919–2001)*

Kafka—*Franz Kafka, a German-speaking Bohemian Jewish novelist and short story writer, widely regarded as one of the major figures of 20th-century literature (1883–1924)*

Kandinsky—*Wassily Kandinsky, Russian painter and art theorist credited with painting one of the first recognized purely abstract works (1866–1944)*

Keller—*Helen Adams Keller, American author, political activist, and lecturer. She was the first deaf-blind person to earn a Bachelor of Arts degree (1880–1968)*

Kerouac—*Jack Kerouac, French-Canadian American novelist and poet (1922–1969)*

Kirkus Reviews

Klee—*Paul Klee, Swiss-born painter, printmaker and draughtsman of German nationality (1879–1940)*

Koestler—*Arthur Koestler, (Arthur Koestler CBE) Hungarian-British journalist, author novels, memoirs and biographies. (1905–1983)*

Krishnamurti—*Jiddu Krishnamurti was an Indian-born philosopher, speaker and writer. In his early life he was groomed to be the new World Teacher but later rejected this mantle and withdrew from the Theosophy organization behind it (1895–1886)*

Kronenberger—*Louis Kronenberger, American literary critic & novelist (1904–1980)*

Kubrick—*Stanley Kubrick, American influential film director, screenwriter, and producer (1928–1999).*

Kundera—*Milan Kundera Kundera, a Czech-born French writer who went into exile in France in 1975, and became a naturalised French citizen in, 1929*

Kung Fu—*Chinese Martial Art*

L

La Bruyère—*Jean de la Bruyère, French philosopher, moralist, and satirist (1645–1696)*

Landers—*Anna Landers (Esther Pauline Lederer) American advice columnist (1918–2002)*

Lamb—*Charles Lamb, English essayist, poet, and antiquarian (1775–1834)*

Langer—*(Susanne Katherina Langer) American philosopher, writer, and educator known for her theories on the influences of art on the mind (1895–1985)*

Lawrence—*(David Herbert Lawrence) English novelist, poet, playwright, essayist, literary critic and painter (1885–1930)*

Lean—*(Sir David Lean, CBE) English film director, producer of large-scale epics, screenwriter and editor (1908–1991)*

Lear—*Norman Lear, American television writer and producer (1922–)*

Le Guin—*Ursula K. Le Guin, American author of novels, children's books, and short stories, mainly in the genres of fantasy and science fiction. She has also written poetry and essays (1929–)*

Lewis—*C.S. Lewis, British novelist, poet born in Belfast, academic, medievalist, literary critic, essayist, lay theologian, broadcaster, lecturer (1898–1963)*

Lippmann—*Walter Lippmann, American writer, reporter, and political commentator (1889–1974)*

London Weekly Review—*1828*

Longfellow—*Henry Wadsworth Longfellow, American poet and educator whose works include "Paul Revere's Ride", The Song of Hiawatha, and Evangeline (1807–1882)*

Lorimer—*George Horace Lorimer, American journalist and author (1867–1937)*

Lynch—*David Keith Lynch, American director, screenwriter, producer, painter, musician, actor, and photographer (1946–)*

M

Mailer—*Norman Mailer (Norman Kingsley) American novelist, journalist, essayist, playwright, filmmaker, actor, and political activist. (1923–2007)*

Mann—*Thomas Mann (Paul Thomas Mann) German novelist, short story writer, social critic, philanthropist, essayist, and the 1929 Nobel Prize in Literature Laureate (1875–1955)*

Marquis—*Don Marquis (Donald Robert Perry Marquis) American humorist, journalist, and author. (1978–1937)*

Maslow—*Abraham Maslow (Abraham Harold Maslow) American psychologist, creator of the Maslow's hierarchy of needs (1908–1970)*

Matisse—*Matisse (Henri Émile Benoît Matisse) French artist, painter, printmaker, and sculptor)1869–1954)*

Mayo—*William James Mayo, American physician and surgeon and one of the founders of the Mayo Clinic (1861–1939)*

Mead—*Margaret Mead, American cultural anthropologist, author and speaker (1901–1978)*

Merrill—*James Merrill, Pulitzer Prize-winning American poet (1926–1995)*

Merton—*Thomas Merton (Thomas Merton, O.C.S.O.) American Catholic writer, theologian and mystic (1915–1968)*

Michelangelo—*Michelangelo, Italian sculptor and painter (1475–1564)*

Mikes—*George Mikes (Mike) Hungarian-born British journalist, humorist and writer (1912–1987)*

Milne—*A.A. Milne (Alan Alexander Milne) English playwright and author, known for his books about the teddy bear Winnie-the-Pooh (1882–1956)*

Milton—*John Milton, English poet, polemicist, man of letters, and civil servant for the Commonwealth of England under Oliver Cromwell (1608–1674)*

Molière—*Molière (Jean-Baptiste Poquelin, known by his stage name Molière) French playwright and actor (1622–1673)*

Mondrian—*Piet Mondrian (Pieter Cornelis "Piet" Mondriaan) Dutch painter and theoretician (1872–1944)*

Monet—*Claude Monet, founder of French Impressionistic painting (1840–1926)*

Moravia—*Alberto Moravia (Alberto Pincherle) Italian novelist and journalist (1907–1990)*

Morrison—*Toni Morrison, American novelist, essayist, editor, teacher & professor emeritus at Princeton University. Winner of Pulitzer Prize and the American Book (1931–)*

Mortimer—*Raymond Mortimer (Charles Raymond Bell Mortimer CBE) British critic on art & literature (1895–1980)*

Mozart—*Wolfgang Amadeus Mozart (baptised as Johannes Chrysostomus Wolfgangus Theophilus Mozart) Austrian prolific and influential composer (1756–1791)*

Munch—*Edvard Munch, was a Norwegian painter and printmaker of psychological themes (1863–1944)*

N

Nabokov—*Vladimir Nabokov, Russian-American novelist (1899–1977)*

Nathan—*George Jean Nathan, American drama critic and magazine editor (1882–1958)*

Neel—*Alice Neel, American visual artist, known for her portraits. (1900–1984)*

Newton, *Isaac Newton, English mathematician & physicist (1642–1727)*

New York Sun—*1918*

Nietzche—*Friedrich Nietzsche, German Philosopher (1844–1900)*

Nin—*Annis Nin (Angela Anaïs Juana Antolina Rosa Edelmira Nin y Culmell) Paris-born American writer, diarist, essayist, novelist, and writer of short stories (1903–1977)*

O

Oates—*Joyce Carol Oates, American writer of novels, plays, novellas, short stories, poetry & nonfiction (1938–)*

Oliver—*Mary Oliver, American poet (1935–)*

O'Keefe—*Georgia O'Keefe (Georgia Totto O'Keeffe) American artist known for her paintings of enlarged flowers, New York skyscrapers,* *and New Mexico landscapes. O'Keeffe has been recognized as the "Mother of American modernism" (1887–1986)*

Osborne—*John Osborne (John James Osborne) English playwright, screenwriter and actor (1929–1994)*

Ozick—*Cynthia Ozick, American novelist (1928–)*

P

Paar—*Jack Paar, American author, radio and television comedian and talk show host (1918–2004)*

Pamuk—*Orhan Pamuk, Turkish writer, novelist, screenwriter, academic and Nobel Laureate (1952–)*

Pasteur—*Louis Pasteur, French biologist, microbiologist and chemist renowned for his discoveries of the principles of vaccination, microbial fermentation and pasteurization (1822–1895)*

Pauling—*Linus Pauling, American biochemist (1901–1994)*

Pavlova—*Anna Pavlova, Russian prima ballerina, principal artist of the Imperial Russian Ballet and the Ballets Russes of Sergei Diaghilev (1881–1931)*

Pepys—*Samuel Pepys, an administrator of the navy of England and Member of Parliament, famous for his diary (1633–1703)*

Peyser—*H.F. Peyser, critic*

Picasso—*Pablo Picasso, Spanish artist lived in France (1881–1973)*

Pissarro—*Camille Pissarro, Danish-French Impressionist and Neo-Impressionist painter of Impressionism and Post-Impressionism (1830–1903)*

Plato—*Plato, ancient Greek philosopher, student of Socrates. (470–399 BCE)*

Poe—*Edgar Allan Poe, American writer, editor, and literary critic best known for his poetry and short stories, tales of mystery and the macabre (1809–1849)*

Poincare—*Henri Poincare, (Jules Henri Poincaré) French mathematician, theoretical physicist, engineer and philosopher of science (1854–1912)*

Pollock—*Jackson Pollock, an American painter and a major figure in the abstract expressionist movement, known for his unique style of drip painting (1912–1956)*

Pope—*Alexander Pope, English poet (1688–1744)*

Pound—*Ezra Pound (Ezra Weston Loomis Pound) Expatriate American poet and critic (1885–1972)*

Prescott—*Peter Prescott, American author and book critic (1935–2004).*

Price—*Luther D. Price, philosopher*

Prokofiev—*Sergey Prokofiev (Sergey Sergeyevich Prokofiev) Russian composer (1891- 1953)*

R

Rauschenberg—*Robert Rauschenberg (Milton Ernest Rauschenberg) American painter and graphic artist (1925–2008)*

Reagan—*Ronald Reagan, actor & 40ᵗʰ President of the United States (1911–1981)*

Renard—*Jules Renard (Pierre-Jules Renard) French writer and member of the Académie Goncourt (1864–1910)*

Richter—*Gerhard Richter, German abstract artist as well as photo-realistic paintings (1932–)*

Rilke—*Rainer Maria Rilke, poet & novelist born in the Austrian, Hungarian Empire (1875–1926)*

Robbins, *Tom Robbins, American novelist (1932–)*

Rodin—*Auguste Rodin (François Auguste René Rodin) French sculptor and progenitor of modern sculpture (1840–1917)*

Roosevelt—*Eleanor Roosevelt, American politician, diplomat, activist and longest-serving First Lady of the United States, (1884–1862)*

Rosten—*Leo Rosten (Leo Calvin Rosten) American humorist, script and short story writer, journalist, Yiddish lexicographer and political scientist (1908–1997)*

Rousseau, *Jean-Jacques Rousseau, rancophone philosopher (1712–1778)*

Ruskin—*John Ruskin, English art critic, art patron & watercolorist (1819–1900)*

Russell—*Bertrand Russell (1872–1970) Bertrand Arthur William Russell, 3rd Earl Russell, OM, FRS was a British philosopher, logician, mathematician, historian, writer, social critic, political activist and Nobel laureate (1872–1970)*

Ryder—*Albert Pinkham Ryder, American painter (1847–1917)*

S

Sagan—*Carl Sagan, American astronomer, cosmologist, astrophysicist, astrobiologist, author, science popularizer, and science communicator (1934–1996)*

Sandburg—*Carl Sandburg Carl August Sandburg was a Swedish-American poet, writer, editor and multiple Pulitzer Prizes winner (1878–1967)*

Santayana—*George Santayana (Jorge Agustín Nicolás Ruiz de Santayana y Borrás,) Spanish philosopher, essayist, poet, and novelist (1863–1952)*

Sayers—*Dorothy Sayers, British novelist, poet and playwright (1893–1957)*

Schank—*Robert C. Schank, American A.I. theorist (1946–)*

Schopenhauer—*Arthur Schopenhauer, German philosopher (1788–1860)*

Schulz—*Charles M. Schulz (Charles Monroe Schulz, nicknamed Sparky) American cartoonist widely known for the comic strip Peanuts (1922–2000)*

Schweitzer—*Albert Schweitzer OM was a French-German theologian, organist, writer, humanitarian, philosopher, and physician and Nobel Laureate (1875–1965)*

Segovia—*Andres Segovia (Andrés Segovia Torres, 1st Marquis of Salobreña) a virtuoso Spanish classical guitarist regarded as one of the greatest guitarists of all time (1893 -1987)*

Seuss—*Dr. Seuss (Theodor Seuss Geisel) an American writer and cartoonist most famous for his children's books (1904–1991)*

Shakespeare—*William Shakespeare (England's national poet and the "Bard of Avon) poet, playwright and actor (1564–1616).*

Shaw—*George Bernard Shaw, Irish playwright, critic, polemicist, and political activist who held both Irish and British citizenship (1856–1950)*

Shaw—*Irwin Shaw (Irwin Shamforoff) American playwright, screenwriter, novelist, and short-story author whose written works have sold more than 14 million (1913–1984)*

Shedd—*John A. Shedd, American writer (1859–1928)*

Shnayerson—*Michael Beahan Shnayerson, American journalist and biographer of Irwin Shaw*

Sibelius—*Jean Sibelius (Johan Julius Christian Sibelius) Finnish composer and violinist (1865–1957)*

Skinner—*B.F. Skinner (Burrhus Frederic Skinner) American psychologist, behaviorist, author, inventor, and social philosopher (1904–1990)*

Sloan—*John Sloan, American artist (1871–1951)*

Smith—*David Smith (Roland David Smith) American abstract expressionist sculptor of large, abstract works, and painter (1906–1965)*

Smith—*W. Eugene Smith, American photojournalist and photo essayist (1918–1978)*

Smithson—*Robert Smithson, American artist, photographer, sculptor (1938–1973)*

Soloviev—*Nicolai Soloviev, Russian composer, music critic and teacher (1846–1916)*

Spender, *Stephen Spender, English poet & novelist (1909–1995)*

Spillane—*Mickey Spillane (Frank Morrison Spillane) American crime novelist, whose stories often feature his signature detective character, Mike Hammer (1918–2006)*

Spolin—*Viola Spolin, American innovator of improvisational techniques, theatre academic, educator and acting coach. (1906–1994)*

Steinbeck—*John Steinbeck (John Ernst Steinbeck, Jr.) American author and Nobel Prize Laureate (1902–1968)*

Steinberg—*Saul Steinberg (cartoonist 1908–1973)*

Stephen—*J.F. Stephen, British High Court judge (1829–1894)*

Stevenson—*Robert Louis Stevenson (Robert Louis Balfour Stevenson) Scottish novelist, poet, essayist, and travel writer (1850–1894)*

Stravinsky—*Igor Stravinsky, Russian composer (1882–1971*

Styron, *William, Styron, American novelist (1925–2006)*

Swami Vivekananda, *Indian Hindu monk and mystic (1863–1902)*

Swift—*Jonathan Swift, Anglo-Irish satirist, essayist, political pamphleteer, poet and cleric (1667–1745)*

T

Tchaikovsky—*Pyotr Ilyich Tchaikovsky, Russian Composer (1840–1893)*

Thackeray—*William Makepeace Thackeray, British novelist and author known for his satirical works, (1811–1863)*

Thatcher—*Margaret Thatcher, Prime Minister of the United Kingdom (1925–2013)*

The Little Red Book *(Alcoholics Anonymous)*

Theroux—*Paul Theroux, (Paul Edward Theroux) an American travel writer and novelist (1041)*

Thomson—*Virgil Thomson, New York Herald Tribune 1940*

Thoreau—*Henry David Thoreau, American essayist, poet, philosopher (1817–1862)*

Thurber—*James Thurber (James Grover Thurber) American cartoonist, author, humorist, journalist, playwright (1894–1961)*

Tocqueville—*(Alexis Charles Henri Clérel, Viscount de Tocqueville) French diplomat, political scientist, and historian (1805–1859)*

Todorov—*Tzvetan Todorov was a Bulgarian-French historian, philosopher, structuralist literary critic, sociologist and essayist and geologist (1939–2017)*

Tolstoy—*Leo Tolstoy (Count Lev Nikolayevich Tolstoy) Russian writer (1828–1910)*

Toscanini—*Arturo Toscanini, acclaimed Italian conductor (1867–1957)*

Trudeau—*Gary Trudeau (Garretson Beekman) American cartoonist, best known for the Doonesbury comic strip. (1948–)*

Twain—*Mark Twain (Samuel Langhorne Clemens) American writer, humorist, entrepreneur, publisher, and lecturer (1835–1910)*

U

Uelsmann—*Jerry Uelsmann, American photographer, and early exponent of photomontage (1934–)*

Ustinov—*Peter Ustinov (Sir Peter Ustinov, CBE FRSA) English writer, actor dramatist, filmmaker, theatre and opera director, stage designer, screenwriter, comedian, humorist, newspaper and magazine columnist, radio broadcaster, and television presenter (1921–2004)*

V

Van der Post—*Sir Laurens van der Post, South African novelist & travel writer, farmer, war hero, political adviser to British heads of government, close friend of Prince Charles, godfather of Prince William (1906–1996)*

Van Gogh—*Vincent van Gogh, Dutch Post-Impressionist painter (1853–1890)*

Villella—*Edward Villella, American ballet dancer and choreographer (1936–)*

Virgil *(Publius Vergilius Maro), Ancient Roman poet of the Augustan period. (70 BC–19 BC)*

Voltaire *(François-Marie Arouet) French Enlightenment writer, historian, and philosopher famous for his wit. (1694–1778)*

Vonnegut—*Kurt Vonnegut, JR, American writer (1922–2007).*

W

Walker—*Alice Walker (Alice Malsenior Walker) American novelist, short story writer, poet, activist, National Book Award and Pulitzer Prize winner (1944–)*

Warren—*Robert Penn Warren was an American poet, novelist, and literary critic and was one of the founders of New Criticism (1905–1989)*

Watson—*Thomas J. Watson Sr, American businessman and chairman and CEO of International Business Machines (IBM) (1914–1956)*

Webster—*Noah Webster, American lexicographer known for his American Spelling Book was instrumental in giving American English a dignity and vitality of its own. (1758–1843)*

Wells—*H.G. Wells, English writer in many genres (1866–1946)*

Whistler—*James Abott McNeill Whistler, American artist (1834–1903)*

White—*E.B. White (Elwyn Brooks) American writer and a world federalist and for more than fifty years, a contributor to The New Yorker magazine (1899–1985)*

Whitman—*Walt Whitman, American poet, essayist, and journalist (1819–1892)*

Wiesel—*Elie Wiesel, Romanian-born American Jewish writer, professor, political activist, Nobel Laureate, and Holocaust survivor (1928–2016)*

Wilde—*Oscar Wilde (Oscar Fingal O'Flahertie Wills Wilde) Irish poet and playwright. (1854–1900)*

Williams, *Tennessee Williams, American playwright (1911–1983)*

Williams—*William Carlos Williams, American poet (modernism and imagism) and physician. (1883–1963)*

Wordsworth—*William Wordsworth English 18th Century Romantic poet (1770 -1850)*

Y

Yellen—*Jack Yellen (Jack Selig Yellen) American lyricist and screenwriter best remembered for writing the lyrics to the songs "Happy Days Are Here Again" (1892–1991)*

Yutang—*Lin Yutang, Chinese writer, translator, linguist and inventor (1895– 1976)*

Quotation Index

A

B

C

Capote, Truman 18, 62
Capra, Frank 17, 62
Carlyle, Thomas 83, 86
Carroll, Lewis 34
Cavett, Dick 89
Chagall, Marc 18
Chandler, Raymond 43
Cheever, John 28, 43
Chinese proverbial wisdom 67
Chinese proverb 13, 33, 34, 63, 67
Churchill, Winston 87

Clancy, Tom 18
Clarke, Sir Arthur Charles 96
Clarke, John 120
Cocteau, Jean 17, 62
Coelho, Paulo 95
Coleridge, Samuel Taylor 56, 84
Copland, Aaron 33, 63
Cousteau, Jacques Yves 34
Coward, Noel 88
Coypel, Antoine 19

D

Dante 121
Daumel, Renee 57, 67
Da Vinci, Leonardo 42
Debussy, Claude 19
de Châteaubriand, François-Rene 19
Degas, Edgar 12
Delacroix, Eugène 35, 49
De Lilo, Don 12
de Mille, Agnes 14
DeMille, Cecil B. 121
Demuth, Charles 35

De Saint-Exupéry, Antoine Marie Jean-Baptiste Roger 19, 23, 57, 121
De San Concordio, Bartolommeo 27
Descartes, René 122
Dillard, R.H.W. 36
Disney, Walt 113
Disraeli, Benjamin 121
Doctorow, E.L. 55
Donne, John) 95
Dryden, John 98
Duchamp, Marcel 35, 73

E

Edison, Thomas 57, 58, 119
Einstein, Albert 8, 31, 36, 37
Eliot, T.S. 56, 124
Ellison, Harlan 9, 105
Emerson, Ralph Waldo 9, 62, 63, 67, 68, 119

Epstein, Jacob 58
Escher, M.C. 57
Evers, Medgar 77
Evening Standard 79

F

Feiffer, Jules 5
Fenton, James 8

Fields, W.C. 59, 120
Fonteyn, Margot 19, 105

K

Kael, Pauline 89
Kafka, Franz 27
Kandinsky, Wassily 33, 69, 70
Keller, Helen Adams 100
Kerouac, Jack 79
Kirkus Reviews 85
Klee, Paul 37, 63, 64, 65

Koestler, Arthur 116
Krishnamurti, Jiddu 28, 56
Kronenberger, Louis 89
Kubrick, Stanley 5, 49
Kundera, Milan 78
Kung Fu, 16

L

La Bruyère, Jean de 108
Landers, Anna 106
Lamb, Charles 86, 92
Langer, Susanne Katherina 22
Lawrence, David Herbert 22
Lean, Sir David 106
Lear, Norman 10
Le Guin, Ursula K. 125

Lewis, C.S. 18, 96
Lippmann, Walter 78
London Weekly Review 79
Longfellow, Henry Wadsworth 5,
    58, 67, 120
Lorimer, George Horace 116
Lynch, David Keith 49, 100, 111

M

Mailer, Norman 41
Mann, Thomas 50
Marquis, Don 20
Maslow, Abraham 76, 102
Matisse, Henri Émile Benoît 24
Mayo, William James 55
Mead, Margaret 104
Merrill, James 52
Merton, Thomas 24, 50
Michelangelo, 104
Mikes, George 108
Milne, A.A. 124

Milton, John 42, 95
Molière, Jean-Baptiste Poquelin
    125
Mondrian, Peit 24, 103
Monet, Claude 103
Moravia, Alberto 23, 51
Morrison, Toni 51
Mortimer, Raymond 86
Mozart, Wolfgang Amadeus 42,
    45
Munch, Edvard 23, 52

N

Nabokov, Vladimir 48, 85
Nathan, George Jean 81
Neel, Alice 47
Newton, Isaac 48

New York Sun 91
Nietzche, Friedrich 81, 85
Nin, Anänis 77

O

P

R

S

90391103R00093

Made in the USA
Middletown, DE
23 September 2018